IMAGES
of America

PORTLAND'S
HAWTHORNE
BOULEVARD

IMAGES
of America

PORTLAND'S HAWTHORNE BOULEVARD

Rhys Scholes

ARCADIA
PUBLISHING

Published by Arcadia Publishing
Charleston, South Carolina

Printed in the United States of America

Library of Congress Control Number: 2020937634

For all general information, please contact Arcadia Publishing:
Telephone 843-853-2070
Fax 843-853-0044
E-mail sales@arcadiapublishing.com
For customer service and orders:
Toll-Free 1-888-313-2665

Visit us on the Internet at www.arcadiapublishing.com

*This book is dedicated to the artists, scientists, workers, and leaders
whose creativity and determination made Hawthorne happen.*

CONTENTS

Acknowledgments   6

Introduction   7

1.   The Early Years   11

2.   Rapid Growth   31

3.   Mid-Century Hawthorne Boulevard   57

4.   Hawthorne Boulevard Reborn   91

5.   21st-Century Hawthorne Boulevard   107

6.   Hawthorne Boulevard Places and People   115

Bibliography   126

ACKNOWLEDGMENTS

It took a big community to make this book happen. Norm Gholston provided counsel, inspiration, and images from his collection. Scott Daniels, Elerina Aldamar, Matthew Cowan, and Robert Warren from the Oregon Historical Society supplied indispensable images and assistance. Brian Johnson and Mary Hansen at the City of Portland Archives found photographs from uncataloged collections.

Hawthorne Boulevard Business Association (HBBA) leaders, past and present, made valuable contributions. Roger Jones and Jan Caplener shared their deep knowledge of Hawthorne. Nancy Chapin, who knows everybody, helped make connections. Dr. Bruce Chaser preserved HBBA images from the 1980s in his attic and loaned me his slide projector so that I could see them.

Terry Baxter at the Multnomah County Archives and Chris Petersen with the Pauling archive at Oregon State University both provided excellent service and images. Val Ballestrem of the Architectural Heritage Center loaned images and coached me regarding architectural styles.

Tim Hills at McMenamins, Emily Brodowicz at Powell's, Bob Howard at Artichoke, Leslie Cole at Grand Central, Greg Moon and Bonnie Ekholm at Western Seminary, Karen Harding of Cup & Saucer, and David A. Martinez of DAM Salsa all contributed images and information.

Beverly Stein and Ruth Gundle gave advice and support. Kristie Duyckinck proofread multiple drafts and provided valuable input. Owen Scholes helped with text and photographs and brought murky images to life. Richard Melling took just-in-time photographs. Carl Abbott inspired me with his great books about Portland and then generously provided advice and valuable suggestions.

I am indebted to the scholarship of Rachel Ann Hardyman whose thesis on Hawthorne was a key source. John Killen's online story about Hawthorne Boulevard in 2015 on the Oregon Live website was inspiring, and historic newspapers, including the *Oregonian*, provided valuable information.

Thanks also to Katy Barber, Emily-Jane Dawson, John Head, Kevin Caplener, Maria Cruz de Lara, Cinnamon Chaser, Steve Einhorn, Ryan Fernandez, Mike Pullen, Mike Crank, Brooke Cabatic, and all the people I missed. Special thanks to Barbara Head for her patience and support.

Thanks to the readers. There are more stories to tell. We can continue the discussion at hawthornebook.com.

INTRODUCTION

There is something contradictory about Hawthorne Boulevard. Shopping is popular, but so is socialism. For visitors, it is a place to see legendary Portland hipness; for neighborhood residents, it is a place to see old friends. Guidebooks accurately report the boulevard's restaurants, pubs, and unique shopping opportunities. Election results for adjacent precincts place locals at the left end of the American political spectrum. The spirit of the street somehow reflects the relatively peaceful coexistence of political correctness and conspicuous consumption.

Observations by guidebook writers are instructive. *Insight Guide* in 1993 said, "Traditionally senior citizens, students and minorities made up the inner-southeast population, but now a growing 'hip' community has moved in, especially along Hawthorne Boulevard." *Moon Guide* in 2004 said the following of Hawthorne Boulevard: "Stores purveying records, fine coffees, secondhand clothing, antiques, crafts and books join cafés and galleries recalling the hip gourmet ghettos of Berkeley, California, and Cambridge, Massachusetts."

How did Hawthorne happen? What are the roots of its reputation? Why did it turn out a little different than other streets? This introduction will provide brief summaries of the history, geography, and economics of Hawthorne and will address the evolution of street names and house numbers. Some political perspectives from the boulevard will also be introduced.

This is primarily a book of photographs and information based on the written record of the past two centuries. The earliest history of this place happened before photography, and the written record is scant and often biased; therefore, a brief review of the life of the place before 1845 is needed.

The first humans to live on the land that became Hawthorne Boulevard arrived many centuries ago. The Multnomah, Kathlamet, Clackamas, Tumwater, and Watlala bands of the Chinook, the Tualatin Kalapuya, and other indigenous nations hunted and traded here.

Pres. Thomas Jefferson sent Lewis and Clark to explore the Northwest in 1804, and one of their assignments was to provide an assessment of the indigenous population. When members of the expedition reached the confluence of the Columbia River and the Willamette River, they estimated there were several thousand native people living in villages scattered along both rivers with a large settlement on Sauvie Island.

Commerce and agriculture were well developed around Portland long before the settlers arrived. Up the Willamette, lamprey and salmon were harvested at Willamette Falls, and above that lay the hunting grounds of the valley. Just down the river was Sauvie Island where large fields of wapato, a root vegetable, were harvested. Up the Columbia River was Celilo Falls where salmon were plentiful and easy to harvest. Chinook and Kalapuyan people traveled to Celilo to meet and trade with Paiute and Nez Perce peoples who lived on the dry side, east of the Cascades.

The west end of the strip of land that became Hawthorne Boulevard was on the east bank of the Willamette River next to a slough. At the spot that became Twelfth Avenue and Hawthorne Boulevard was a powerful freshwater spring at the head of the slough. Tribal members traveling along the river might have paddled up the slough and stopped there.

The villages that Lewis and Clark saw were not there 30 years later. The Europeans brought diseases for which the native people had no immunity. Between 1800 and 1850, a total of 90 percent of the indigenous people in the Northwest died from malaria, small pox, and other diseases. The tribal folk who survived were displaced from their ancestral lands, and many were sent to reservations. Into the 21st century, the descendants of these native people are still working to protect their heritage and regain some of what they have lost.

The first white settler came in 1827, but he did not stay long. Later, James Stephens, who came in 1845, filed a donation land claim and laid out the streets for the city of East Portland (1870–1890). Stephens donated seven acres of his claim to be used for a mental hospital, run by Dr. James C. Hawthorne. That asylum was built on the banks of the slough next to the spring. The slough took the name "Asylum Slough," and it was fed by "Asylum Springs." Caring for people in need became the boulevard's first industry as Dr. Hawthorne's mental hospital was the largest employer in the old city of East Portland.

By the time the first bridge across the Willamette River was opened, East Portland was already experiencing rapid growth. The 25-foot-deep canyons cut by Asylum Slough prevented development on dozens of blocks for several decades. Years of dredging and filling dramatically changed the topography of Southeast Portland west of Twelfth Avenue. Land for new homes was created, but a beautiful park was lost.

At the start of the 20th century, Portland was growing rapidly. The Lewis and Clark Exposition in 1905 brought thousands of visitors to Oregon, and many of them decided to stay. Since the land on the west side was filling up, the preponderance of new residential growth shifted to the east side where expanding streetcar lines served the new developments. By 1910, Portland had more residents on the east side than on the west. As the automobile became popular, car dealers and gas stations proliferated along Hawthorne in the 1920s.

Throughout the 20th century, merchants and residents organized to make Hawthorne better. They sponsored parades, fairs, and festivals while fighting for parks, sidewalks, and streetlights. When problems of poverty and dilapidated buildings grew in the 1960s and 1970s, neighbors created agencies and associations to fight back. In the 1980s, a new wave of businesses arrived on Hawthorne Boulevard, and a new business association partnered with neighborhoods and city government for community improvement. This revitalization of Hawthorne Boulevard helped coalesce its special character. However, the roots of Hawthorne Boulevard's identity can be found in earlier decades as well.

This book tells the story of the evolution of Hawthorne by sharing images and events from bygone years. Along the way, it looks for the roots of Hawthorne Boulevard's modern character. Hawthorne Boulevard has had many names. It was U Street when James Stephens drew the first plat for East Portland. He used letters to designate the east-west streets from A (now Glisan Street) on the north to U on the south. Later, it became Asylum Avenue. In 1888, leaders of the City of East Portland changed the name to Hawthorne Avenue. It became Hawthorne Boulevard in 1933 when a citywide plan was enacted to rationalize Portland addresses and make them more consistent.

Until 1933, the addresses on Hawthorne were numbered sequentially, starting at the river, without regard to cross streets. Since 1933, the addresses have been tied to the numbered north-south streets that the boulevard intersects. For example, the Holman's Funeral Home address was 828 Hawthorne Avenue before the change and 2610 Hawthorne Boulevard after 1933.

Another change in 1933 was the addition of a prefix to all of the street names in the city. Every address in Portland has capital letters between the number and the name in order to place it in one of the city's six quadrants: North (N), Northeast (NE), Southeast (SE), South (S), Southwest (SW), and Northwest (NW). (Mathematicians may wince, but Portlanders are unapologetic about their six quadrants.) Since almost every street mentioned in this book would carry the letters "SE," they have been omitted. The title of this book could be *Portland's SE Hawthorne Boulevard*, and intersections with SE Grand Avenue or SE Twelfth Avenue could be described in that way. They are not. Readers are strongly advised, however, that these are the correct names of these streets, and they are often required for successful navigation in Portland.

Most of the streets that intersect Hawthorne Boulevard are numbered avenues, but several important ones have names. The street that was originally Fourth Avenue became Union Avenue and then became Martin Luther King Jr. Boulevard. The street that was Fifth Avenue became Grand Avenue. These two one-way streets are officially US Highway 99 East, and before the construction of Interstate 5, it was the principal north-south highway on the West Coast.

Geographically, Grand Avenue is at the top of the first hill as you travel east from the river. Below Grand Avenue, coming up from Water Avenue and First Street, the ground was marshy or underwater in the early days. For many years, parts of Hawthorne ran on an elevated wooden roadway as did many of the streets in the neighborhood. Chapter two will tell the story of filling the lowlands. Chapter three will show the burial of that neighborhood under bridge ramps. The intersection of Grand Avenue and Hawthorne Boulevard figures in several stories.

Seven blocks farther from the river, Twelfth Avenue shares an intersection with Ladd Avenue, which intersects at a 45-degree angle marking the northwest corner of Ladd's Addition. This corner was important because of Hawthorne Springs and Hawthorne Park, which were nearby. The topography on Hawthorne Avenue below Twelfth Avenue went through many human-caused changes between 1850 and 1915.

Hawthorne Boulevard continues uphill and, at Twentieth Avenue, intersects Elliott Avenue at the northeast corner of Ladd's Addition, a unique neighborhood of diagonal streets and rose gardens and a recognized historic district. The neighborhood to the north here is called Buckman. On the south is the Hosford-Abernethy neighborhood, which includes Ladd's Addition.

Nine blocks farther, with some steep elevation gain, the top of the hill is reached at Twenty-eighth Avenue.

Above Thirtieth Avenue is the district with the greatest concentration of storefront retail businesses and the area that is most frequently identified as "Hawthorne." When Rachel Ann Hardyman studied Hawthorne Boulevard gentrification for her 1992 master's thesis in geography at Portland State University, she focused on the area from Twenty-eighth Avenue to Thirty-ninth Avenue because the phenomena she was investigating was most in evidence there. The Sunnyside neighborhood is north of Hawthorne Boulevard here, and Richmond is to the south.

Thirty-seventh Avenue and Hawthorne Boulevard serves as an unofficial center of the neighborhood. The Bagdad Theater is there, and in both directions, an almost unbroken line of shops and eateries extends for several blocks. The five blocks from Thirty-fourth Avenue to Thirty-ninth Avenue have the highest concentration of vintage storefronts with maximum pedestrian appeal. In 2009, the name of Thirty-ninth Avenue was changed to Cesar Chavez Boulevard.

Above Chavez Boulevard, there is still a dense business district that is entirely walkable, but there are many newer buildings and more parking lots.

Hawthorne Boulevard starts to climb Mount Tabor at Fiftieth Avenue. The streetcar tracks turned south at this point, and modern bus transit continues that tradition. At Fifty-fifth Avenue, the street jogs right around the historic mansion, built on the site of the Prettyman cabin and, later, home to a seminary.

At Sixtieth Avenue, Hawthorne disappears into Mount Tabor Park. Although it reappears sporadically above Seventieth Avenue, it is purely residential in those areas and beyond the scope of this book.

The economic geography of neighborhood near Hawthorne Boulevard has changed over the years. Sunnyside was built to be a middle-class suburb. Colonial Heights had covenants that required larger homes and pure-white residents. The north side of Ladd's Addition, near the Hawthorne Boulevard streetcar, developed first and included many large, expensive houses. Southern Ladd's Addition, developed later, was affordable to working-class families and attracted many Italian and Asian immigrants.

In the 1930s, the Home Owners Loan Corporation published maps that color-coded urban neighborhoods to guide the decisions of loan officers. All of the Buckman neighborhood and half of Richmond were coded red, meaning home loans were unavailable or came at very high interest rates. The Colonial Heights area south of Hawthorne Boulevard and the Mount Tabor neighborhood above Fiftieth Avenue were colored blue, which was the second-highest rating. The other areas near Hawthorne were colored yellow for average, but none were colored green for ritziest.

In the 21st century, the price of homes in all of the neighborhoods near Hawthorne Boulevard is beyond the means of middle-income homebuyers. The rapid construction of new apartments may moderate rents in some older buildings.

The racial makeup of Hawthorne Boulevard was shaped in the early years by overt prejudice. In 1857, when a statewide vote was held to adopt a constitution, the ballot included two additional questions. On one, 75 percent of Oregonians voted to oppose slavery in the territory. On the other, 85 percent opposed allowing "free negroes" to live in Oregon. Black exclusion laws were in effect (but seldom enforced) well into the 20th century.

People from China, East India, and Hawaii were all victims of intense and sometimes brutal discrimination in early Oregon, but many of these new immigrants played critical roles in building the homes and cities of the white settlers. Much of the land where homes and businesses now stand along Hawthorne Boulevard was cleared by Chinese laborers. Some of these Chinese laborers were cleared from the land by a white mob in 1886. That story is in chapter one.

Parts of Hawthorne Boulevard have been poor, and parts have been prosperous, and the last two decades of the 20th century were a period of increasing prosperity in all of them. Did Hawthorne Boulevard experience gentrification in the 1980s and 1990s?

Rachel Hardyman's 1992 thesis, "Hawthorne Boulevard: Commercial Gentrification and the Creation of an Image," dives deep into the contradictions between local capitalism and progressive values. She found that gentrification, using a standard academic definition, was happening during the 1980–1992 period that she studied. She also found that cultural movements, including feminism and lesbian/gay rights, have helped to shape the place that Hawthorne Boulevard has become. Chapter four will tell some of these stories.

In 2018, *Fodors* said, "This eclectic commercial thoroughfare was at the forefront of Portland's hippie and LGBT scenes in the '60s and '70s. As the rest of Portland's East Side has become more urbane and popular among hipsters, young families, students, and the so-called creative class over the years, Hawthorne has retained an arty, homegrown flavor."

Hardyman's analysis focuses on small business and deliberately avoids chain retailers. This book, on the other hand, includes many photographs of Fred Meyer stores and production facilities. The author has not colluded with this company nor received any compensation for brand promotion. Rather readers benefit from Meyer's habit of hiring professional photographers to document all aspects of his operations and from the subsequent donation of that massive collection of photographs to the Oregon Historical Society.

The first five chapters of this book present Hawthorne Boulevard history in approximate chronological order. The sixth chapter includes stories that do not fit neatly into the chronology. Two buildings that have had changing uses over many years begin the chapter. The book ends with stories of three people whose lives illuminate parts of the essence of Hawthorne Boulevard.

How did Hawthorne happen? The creative tension between capitalism and anticapitalism is easy to identify. The influences of art and science are apparent. The opportunity that cheap commercial rent presented to counterculture veterans who then became successful entrepreneurs as their community evolved to embrace higher values is clearly part of the story. Geography is important as well.

Take a walk on Hawthorne Boulevard and listen carefully for the sound of a different drum.

One

THE EARLY YEARS

Historic Hawthorne Boulevard begins on the bank of the Willamette River and goes east about three miles to Mount Tabor, a dormant volcano. In geologic time, this land is very new. Mount Tabor last erupted about 300,000 years ago, and the shape of the landscape continued to be changed by massive ice age floods and periodic subduction zone earthquakes.

The city of Portland traces its history to a series of events on the west side of the Willamette and a spot called "the clearing" where white settlers laid out a successful townsite. The river was deep enough at that point that oceangoing vessels coming up the Columbia River to the Willamette River could dock and transact business. The bank was high enough that the clearing was above the annual floodwaters in most years. From their townsite, people could see the marshy land across the river, snowcapped Mount Hood in the distance, and Mount Tabor in between.

Most of the east side was a low-lying plain with a wetland near the river subject to seasonal flooding. Glacial action thousands of years earlier and natural springs over the centuries had carved deep creeks and sloughs.

On the west side, the hills are close to the river and subject to landslides. The last subduction zone earthquake was in 1700. Over the course of the centuries, the path of the Willamette River has moved. Perhaps, the previous quakes helped to create the west side clearing and the east side wetlands. Perhaps, the next earthquake will set a new table.

The first white settler on the land that is now Portland built his cabin on the east side of the river in 1827. Etienne Lucier, and later Basil Poirer (another French Canadian), lived there. John McLoughlin, as executor of Poirer's estate, sold the land to James B. Stephens, who had arrived on an early wagon train.

Two years later, naturopathic doctor Perry Prettyman staked a claim two miles east. In 1850, he built a house on the slopes of Mount Tabor with a view down toward the river. As more settlers came, Stephens built a ferry across the river, and Prettyman cleared a road down to the ferry. The name of that road would change several times over the next 80 years, but it is known today as Hawthorne Boulevard.

A Kalapuya man.

A native of Oregon.

The image at left, titled "A Kalapuya Man," is from an engraving by Alfred T. Agate who was part of the Wilkes Expedition in 1841. It portrays a survivor of the disease epidemics that decimated his people. Historian David Williams, writing in the *Oregon Encyclopedia*, says, "By the 1840's, few Kalapuyans remained in the region. Where their population at one time was an estimated 25,000 people, perhaps a few thousand remained at the time of the Wilkes Expedition." The traditional homeland of the Kalapuyan peoples stretched from the Tualatin River near Portland to the Umpqua River south of Eugene. The Chinook people had longhouses along the Columbia River from the Pacific Ocean up to the Dalles and one at Willamette Falls in Oregon City. The image below is an engraving by Richard W. Dodson from a sketch by Alfred T. Agate. It shows a Chinook lodge with a sunken central fire pit. The Cathlapotle Plankhouse is a modern-day reconstruction of a traditional Chinook structure, and it can be visited at the Ridgefield, Washington, National Wildlife Refuge about 25 miles from Portland. (Both, Library of Congress.)

Etienne Lucier was a voyageur and the first white settler in Portland, building a cabin for his family on the east side in 1827. The painting above, *Running the Rapids* by Frances Anne Hopkins, shows voyageurs in action. Lucier came west with the Wilson Price Hunt Expedition in 1810, sent by wealthy New York capitalist John Jacob Astor to support his new fur-trading post as chronicled in Peter Stark's magnificent book *Astoria*. The exact location of Lucier's cabin is in dispute, but it was close to the place that became Hawthorne Boulevard. (Library and Archives Canada.)

John McLoughlin, pictured at right, was the chief factor of the Columbia Department of the Hudsons Bay Company (HBC) and presided over the company's outpost at Fort Vancouver on the Columbia River just north of Portland. When Etienne Lucier left Portland with his wife and children and settled in French Prairie (about 25 miles south on the Willamette River), Lucier's "squatter's claim" passed to Basil Poirer, a retired cook at Fort Vancouver. When Poirer died, McLoughlin became executor of his will. In 1845, he sold the Lucier/Poirer squatter's claim to James Stephens for $200. (Oregon Historical Society, ba000846.)

James B. Stephens

James "Jimmy" Bowles Stephens arrived in Oregon by wagon train with his family in 1844. He could have been a founder of the Portland townsite on the west side in 1845 when William Overton offered to sell him 320 acres of what became downtown Portland for $300 (or 300 salmon barrels; accounts differ). Stephens declined and bought the east side land instead. His father, Emor Stephens, was Pres. Thomas Jefferson's nephew and was the first person buried, in 1846, in what became Lone Fir Cemetery. Jimmy and his wife, Elizabeth, are buried there as well. (Oregon Historical Society, OrHi 25655.)

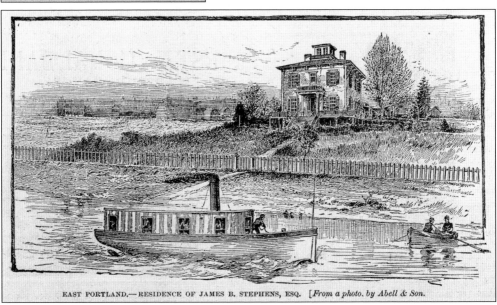

EAST PORTLAND.— RESIDENCE OF JAMES B. STEPHENS, ESQ. [*From a photo. by Abell & Son.*]

The passage of the Donation Claim Act allowed James and Elizabeth Stephens to gain uncontested legal ownership of 640 acres extending from today's Oak Street to Division Street, from the river to Twentieth Avenue. Their home is pictured. Stephens established the first ferry across the Willamette in 1846 with a small rowboat and expanded to a ferry propelled by a horse on a treadmill as traffic increased. He laid out the lots in 1850 that became the city of East Portland and donated seven acres for an insane asylum to be operated by Dr. J.C. Hawthorne and by Stephens's son-in-law Dr. A.M. Loryea. (Oregon Historical Society, OrHi31910.)

Jimmy and Elizabeth Stephens were married in the frontier town of Cincinnati, Ohio, in 1830 and enjoyed 57 years of a close partnership until 1887, when Elizabeth passed away. Jimmy, at 81, deeply mourned her loss and commissioned this unusual grave marker. On the back of the marker, Jimmy left the following message: "Here we lie by consent. After 57 years 2 months and 2 days sojourning through life awaiting natures immutable laws to return us back to the elements of the universe of which were first composed." As a whole, the marker embraces art, science, and love. Generations of visitors to the Lone Fir Cemetery have seen this stone, and perhaps, some have been touched by it. Perhaps, this is an early influence on the character of the community. (Author's collection.)

Dr. J.C. Hawthorne was born in Pennsylvania in 1819 and received medical training in Kentucky. He moved to Auburn, California, in 1850 where he practiced medicine and served in the California State Senate. Dr. Hawthorne came to Portland in 1856 and operated Multnomah County's hospital and poor farm. In 1862, he and Dr. Loryea were the only bidders when Gov. A.C. Gibbs sought a contractor for Oregon's first mental health facility. In 1869, Dorothea Dix, a leader in the movement to reform mental health, visited the facility and praised the care provided there. (Oregon Historical Society, OrHi 746.)

The asylum was built on a west sloping hillside bordering the slough. Visitors remarked on the beauty and tranquility of the property. The rates that the doctors charged the state and the consequent cost to the taxpayers was a source of controversy. Dr. Hawthorne was strategic in his contributions to elected officials and was thus an effective lobbyist. When Oregon legislators raised concerns about the excessive cost of Dr. Hawthorne's facility, he traveled to the state capitol in Salem, and the funding was continued. (Oregon Historical Society, bb007037.)

When Dr. Loryea lost his fortune in the bank crash of 1873, he moved on to other pursuits, and Dr. S.E. Josephi became Hawthorne's partner in the asylum. After Hawthorne died in 1881, Josephi and Hawthorne's widow, Rachel, continued the operation of the facility. But without Dr. Hawthorne's lobbying, the state opened its own mental health hospital in Salem in 1883. The asylum building was destroyed by fire in 1888. Josephi went on to be dean of the University of Oregon School of Medicine and serve two terms as an Oregon state senator. (Gholston Collection.)

S.E.JOSEPHI,M.D.,
PORTLAND,OR.

Rachel Louise Hite married J.C. Hawthorne in 1865, and they had two daughters, Catherine and Louise. After Dr. Hawthorne's death in 1881, Rachel Hawthorne managed the Hawthorne estate's properties. The Hawthornes were both successful real estate developers who acquired and subdivided large tracts of land in East Portland. Rachel Hawthorne owned the properties until she died in 1912. (Oregon Historical Society, OrHi 38379.)

There are many natural springs in East Portland, and the one at Twelfth Avenue and Hawthorne is among the largest. In 1888, the East Portland Water Company used this spring, which could produce a million gallons of water a day, to serve the local community. The outflow fed Asylum Slough whose path wound through East Portland, creating ponds and streams and requiring the construction of multiple trestles and elevated roadways. It is difficult to imagine how this land looked before it was filled. Ravines and open water hindered travel and impeded development. (Oregon Historical Society, OrHi 92631.)

Asylum Slough meets the Willamette River in this view from the 1870s. It shows the trestle for what is now Martin Luther King Jr. Boulevard crossing the slough. Another trestle can be seen in the distance. The photograph was taken near what is now the intersection of Oak Street and Sixth Avenue. (Oregon Historical Society, bb00560.)

A portion of an 1865 photograph from the west hills above Portland looking east shows a large area of open water near the river. The buildings among the trees were on a bluff about a quarter of a mile from the river and probably were on the street that became Grand Avenue. The clump of trees between the river and slough is visible near the left of the image. (Gholston Collection.)

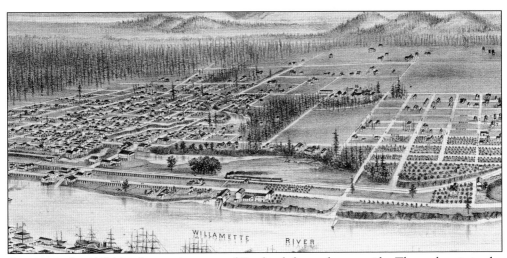

A section of an 1881 bird's-eye view map of Portland shows the east side. The asylum is in the right center with the number 16 above it. Asylum Slough is visible, as is the area of water (above and left from the train) that came to be known as the frog pond. Note that the railroad crosses on one trestle, and Water Avenue crosses another. The train is about to pass the clump of trees referenced in the previous images. The easternmost intersection on Asylum Street is at Twentieth Avenue. The Prettyman house is up in the trees. (Oregon Historical Society, bb008845.)

DR. P. PRETTYMAN.

Dr. Perry Prettyman and his family joined the wagon train led by William McKinney that arrived in Oregon in 1847. They traveled with the Luelling family, who sold fruit trees to early Oregonians. After surveying possible sites from the Puget Sound to Southern Oregon, he and his wife filed their donation land claim on the west side of Mount Tabor. Dr. Prettyman was born in Delaware in 1796 and studied at the Botanic Medical School in Baltimore. He imported dandelion seeds from Missouri due to their medicinal properties and first cultivated them on Mount Tabor. He died in 1872. (Author's collection.)

H.W. Prettyman was five years old when he traveled from Missouri to Oregon with his parents. He grew up in the forest on Mount Tabor and recalled shooting deer from the front porch of his parents' house. The Prettymans' original claim went from the Baseline Road (now Stark Street) to the Section Road (now Division Street) and from Thirty-ninth Avenue (now Cesar Chavez Avenue) to Sixtieth Avenue. Perry Prettyman's granddaughter Mary Elizabeth Prettyman Williams was born on the 1,000-acre family farm. In a 1961 article in the *Portland Reporter*, she recalled that the land was cleared by Chinese labor. (Oregon Historical Society, PF 882 02001 001.)

H. W. Prettyman, 1847.

Prettyman built this 70-foot-long, two-story house out of cedar logs with a stone foundation. In the upper story, there was a large room where the pioneer community gathered for meetings and sometimes dances. Located at what is now Fifty-fifth Avenue and Hawthorne Boulevard, the spot was at a junction of trails to the Columbia River, Portland, and Oregon City. Dr. Prettyman was known to welcome travelers. Phillip Buehner purchased the property in the 1890s and, eventually, built a mansion there. (Oregon Historical Society, OrHi 85517.)

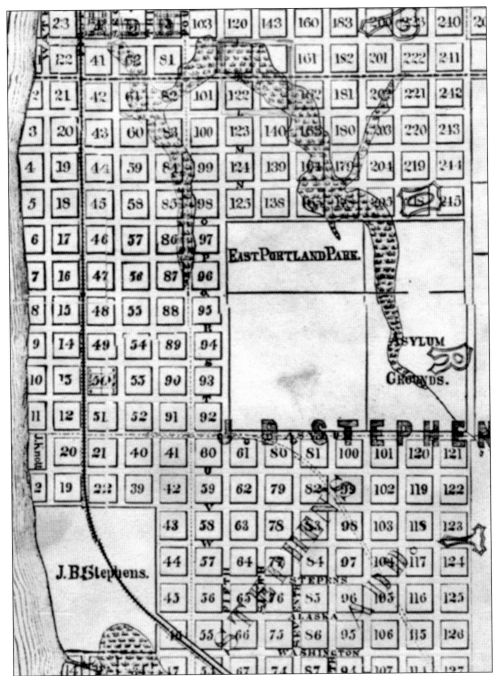

In this 1874 map, East Portland Park and the asylum grounds are just north of Asylum Street, between Fifth Avenue (now Grand) and Twelfth Avenue. Water flowed from the springs in a northwesterly direction, widening as it passed the asylum buildings. Several arms of the slough reached up through low sections of East Portland until they reached the Willamette River. The railroad tracks running north to south two blocks from the river were on raised land or trestles as was Water Avenue one block west. A trestle for Fifth Avenue crossed the slough. (Oregon Historical Society, bb007853.)

Isaiah Amos moved to Oregon in 1887 and quickly became a leader in the Prohibition cause. He ran for mayor of Portland, state senator, and other offices as a candidate of the Prohibition Party. His former home at 2709 Hawthorne is pictured in this undated *Oregon Journal* photograph. The Queen Anne–style house features an octagonal turret with matching dormer and spindle work accenting the wraparound porch. It was diagonally across Hawthorne and Twenty-sixth Avenues from the Burrell Mansion and would have commanded an excellent view to the west. (Photograph courtesy of the *Oregonian*; Oregon Historical Society, OrHi 49085.)

James B. Stephens's first ferry across the Willamette was a rowboat from the riverbank next to his home. Later, he had a larger ferry that left the east side from the foot of Taylor Street. Finally, Stephens built an improved landing at the foot of Oak Street where the Stark Street Ferry, pictured here, took its name from its west side landing. In this view of the ferry departing from the east side, a wagon carrying firewood from the east to the west can be seen. (Oregon Historical Society, ba004728.)

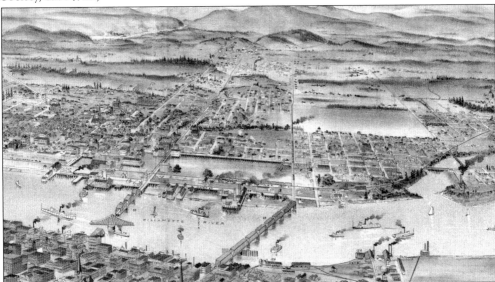

This 1890 map shows that much of the east side near the river was still a marsh. In the middle of the image, Fifth Avenue (later Grand Avenue) is raised on posts between Morrison and Hawthorne Avenues east of the swamp. Moving inland there are houses south of Hawthorne until Twelfth Avenue where a large empty pasture awaits the development of Ladd's Addition. North of Hawthorne the land is clear from Ninth to Sixteenth Avenues where the asylum stood earlier. Asylum Slough is marked by a line of trees crossing Hawthorne Avenue at Twelfth Avenue. (Library of Congress.)

This image shows a Chinese man selling firewood in Portland in the 1880s. Chinese immigrants provided much of the labor that made white settlement possible, but there was a substantial minority of whites who were openly and violently bigoted. In the early morning hours of March 5, 1886, about 125 Chinese men were driven out of their shacks on Mount Tabor by 50 masked white men. The *Oregonian* reported that Chinese men were forced down to the Albina ferry and compelled to cross the river. (Oregon Historical Society, OrHi 23349.)

The Chinese woodcutters would have found a welcome but not a lot of sleeping space in Portland's Chinatown. Stretched along Second Avenue as a buffer between the docks and the more affluent section of town, Chinatown was full of single Chinese men who were often crowded into upstairs sleeping rooms. Just two weeks before the incident on Mount Tabor, Chinese workers at a woolen mill in Oregon City had been evicted by a white mob. (Oregon Historical Society, OrHi 45487.)

The Brown Hotel and Apartments was a five-story building located on the northwest corner of Hawthorne and Grand Avenues. It was built by A.D. Brown in 1892 at a reported cost of $90,000. In 1906, the newly organized East Side Club leased the top floor and converted apartments to reading, smoking, and club rooms. (Gholston Collection.)

The Baltimore Hotel opened at 303 Hawthorne Avenue at the corner of Water Avenue in 1891. The Eastside Music Hall next door hosted meetings of the People's Party in 1896. The image features four men and a dog. At right is a police officer standing alone. On either side of the door are men who might be the storekeeper and bartender. The dog waits patiently in front of the door, and to the left is a man in front of a barrel. Weinhard's beer, a local brew, is advertised. (Gholston Collection.)

This undated photograph shows the East Side Bowling Hall with its employees and patrons. The two young men on the steps were likely the pinsetters. While several saloons had bowling alleys on their premises, competitive team bowling was the province of the elites. Both the Multnomah Amateur Athletic Club and the Arlington Club had alleys as part of their spacious downtown clubhouses. In the 1890s, the clubs battled furiously for the city championship and contested with their peer clubs around the Puget Sound. (Gholston Collection.)

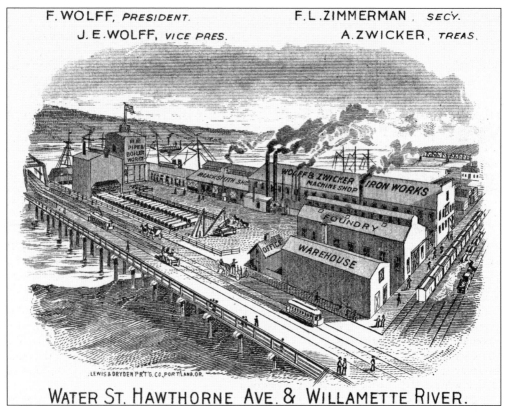

F. WOLFF, PRESIDENT. F.L.ZIMMERMAN, SEC'Y.
J.E.WOLFF, VICE PRES. A.ZWICKER, TREAS.

WATER ST. HAWTHORNE AVE. & WILLAMETTE RIVER.

Wolff & Zwicker Ironworks was the successor to a firm that started on the west side of Portland in 1869. In 1893, it moved to the west end of Hawthorne Avenue by the river. In this illustration from the company's billhead, the Madison Street Bridge is visible at far left, and streetcars, pedestrians, and horses travel the elevated portion of Hawthorne Avenue next to the ironworks. The railroad line can be seen at right, and the Morrison Street Bridge is in the distance. Wolff & Zwicker produced iron jail bars for the Oregon State Penitentiary, boilers, fire escapes, and water mains for Portland and other communities. (Gholston Collection.)

Phillip Buehner, an engineer born in Illinois and educated in Missouri, joined the firm briefly in the mid-1880s when it manufactured the pipe to carry water to Portland from the Bull Run reservoir on the slopes of Mount Hood. This photograph shows that Buehner's name has been added, and on the left, boats are under construction. Wolff & Zwicker built torpedo boats and light ships for the federal government. Buehner purchased the Prettyman property at Fifty-fifth and Hawthorne Avenues and built a mansion there, which is seen in the next chapter. (Gholston Collection.)

Dredge No. 1 was built for the St. Louis–based Missouri-Alaska Dredging and Mining Co. by Joseph Supple at his shipyard just north of Wolff & Zwicker. The 100-foot-long light draft boat was equipped with a continuous chain of 36 buckets that could be deployed to depths of 4 to 40 feet to scrape sand from the river bottoms. The buckets emptied into sluice boxes where the sand was sprayed with water at high pressure to separate the gold. After the dredge was completed in 1898, it went to the Yukon. (Gholston Collection.)

November 1, 1893, was cold and foggy, and the motorman for the trolley *Inez* accelerated up the grade to the Madison Street Bridge to gain momentum on the icy tracks. Because of the fog, he did not see the red signal indicating an open span until he was on the bridge, and then, the brakes failed to slow the car on the slippery tracks. Seven of the 18 passengers perished when the trolley plunged into the Willamette River. The photograph shows the trolley on a barge after it was pulled from the water. (Oregon Historical Society, PF1906.)

On July 5, 1880, the Jefferson Street Ferry began service to U Street on the east side of the river. In July 1888, a herd of steer was crossing on the ferry, and one fell through a ventilation hole in the deck and began a five-hour reign of terror in cramped quarters below next to a hot boiler. After other options were exhausted, the unfortunate steer was shot, and butchers came to extricate him. In this image, the Morrison Street Bridge is downriver, and underneath it, the Stark Street Ferry is visible mid-river. (Gholston Collection.)

By the end of the 19th century, Portland had grown, but the Stephens house was still by the water. When it was moved uphill to SE Twelfth Avenue in 1902 to make room for more railroad tracks, it lost its cupola. The house is in the National Register of Historic Places. (Gholston Collection.)

Two

Rapid Growth

Portland's business leaders organized the 1905 Lewis and Clark Exposition to promote the city's growth, and their dreams came true. In his book *The Great Extravaganza*, historian Carl Abbott refers to the exposition as "the onset of the greatest economic boom that Portland had ever experienced." He reports that the east side population grew from 32,000 to 178,000 between 1900 and 1916. Portland "built a new middle-class city on the east side of the Willamette," Abbott observed.

The exposition was almost held in Hawthorne Park, which included the old asylum grounds, but Guilds Lake in Northwest Portland was ultimately chosen. Hawthorne Park hosted large meetings, concerts, church services, and family picnics around the turn of the century. Visitors remarked on the natural beauty of the park, which was so close to the center of the city. A few years later, in spite of neighborhood resistance, the trees had been uprooted, and the pond was buried under 20 feet of fill to make 10 more blocks for residential development.

Near the river, filling of low ground moved more quickly as the value of the newly created land increased. With other centrally located lots already developed, the sale value of the marshy and flooded lots made the filling worthwhile. Fill was mined on the north side of Mount Tabor, but even more came from dredging the channel in the river. Trestles were eliminated as the land was raised for streets, sometimes creating a waffle pattern where lots had not yet been filled.

As automobiles replaced streetcars, gas stations were built all along Hawthorne Avenue. With multiple car dealers, garages, and related businesses, Hawthorne and Grand Avenues together became "Auto Row."

The Lewis and Clark Exposition was a big party, and people came from around the world to have a good time. Presumably, people who did not want to have a good time stayed home. Possibly, the people who decided not only to visit but also to move to Portland were those who most enjoyed the party, and many of those people settled around Hawthorne Avenue. In a search for the antecedents of Hawthorne Boulevard's reputation, this cannot be overlooked.

The Lewis and Clark Exposition brought hundreds of thousands of visitors to Portland. Civic leaders planned the exposition to encourage investors and new residents for the city, and the exhibits showcased the wonders of life in the Pacific Northwest. The strategy was successful, and Hawthorne Avenue was one of the places that experienced rapid population growth after the exposition. This image shows opening day festivities in 1905. (Photograph by Fred Kiser; Oregon Historical Society, ba018041.)

A GROUP OF WORKERS

CHURCH OF GOD

FAITH GOSPEL HOME
430 Hawthorne Ave. Portland, Ore.
HOME PHONE B 1409

The Church of God held a 10-day general assembly in 1905 in its meetinghouse at 430 Hawthorne Avenue. Congregants slept in the upper two stories and ate in the basement. According to an *Oregonian* account, "As the building was not completed, such of the elders and other saints as happened to be carpenters have worked on the building during the day and preached at night." (Gholston Collection.)

Here, Portlanders turn out to view the smoldering aftermath of the Madison Street Bridge fire on June 22, 1902. Six blocks of riverfront and the east end of the bridge were destroyed by the fire, which started at the Phoenix Ironworks and was fueled by the Standard Oil Company's tanks nearby. The size and complexity of this fire hastened the purchase of specially designed boats with steam-powered pumps to better combat such conflagrations in the future. This was the second wooden bridge connecting Hawthorne Avenue on the east side with Madison Street on the west. It was repaired after the fire and then replaced in 1910 with a metal bridge. (Oregon Historical Society, CN 003977.)

Minnie Hubbard operated this grocery store at the corner of Forty-third and Hawthorne Avenues during the first decade of the 20th century. She and her husband, plumber Richard W. Hubbard, lived next door. (Oregon Historical Society, OrgLot1044.)

In 1905, Hubbard had the only grocery store on Hawthorne Avenue east of Seventh Avenue, but competition grew in the subsequent years as nearby lots were purchased and houses built. By 1914, there were more than a dozen groceries east of Twentieth Avenue. (Oregon Historical Society, bb011869.)

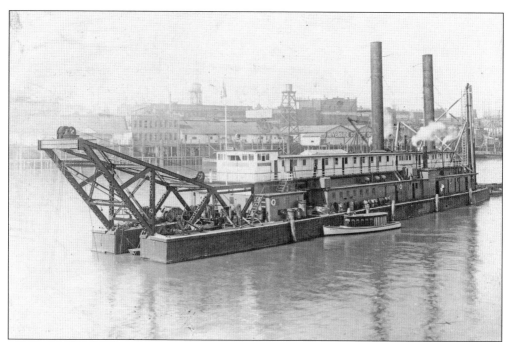

On January 12, 1865, the City of Portland imposed a special property tax of one half of one percent in order to fund the purchase of a dredging machine to deepen the river for navigation while using the dredge spoils to fill wetlands and sloughs. In 1891, the Port of Portland was created by the Oregon legislature to deepen the Willamette River channel in order to allow large oceangoing vessels to dock. Pictured above is the Port of Portland's dredge *Columbia*. In the image below, workers assemble large pipes to transport dredge spoils. (Both, Gholston Collection.)

In the image above, dredge spoils are carried to a station on the bank, and the fill is hauled to where it is needed. In the image below, fill is pumped directly to the riverbank. The mouth of Asylum Slough was filled in 1906. Much of the work was done by the Pacific Bridge Company, which was the only bidder for some of the projects. Some of the fill came from the river, but many tons came from a gravel quarry that Pacific Bridge Company operated on the north slope of Mount Tabor; there, neighbors were increasingly concerned about the growing hole. The quarry was on the north side of Villa Avenue (now Glisan Avenue) between present-day Sixty-third and Sixty-seventh Avenues. The fill was transported three miles west in special cars on the Montavilla streetcar line and used to raise the level of the streets near the river. In 1907, William Ladd signed a contract on behalf of himself and other landowners to fill 18 blocks between Hawthorne and Belmont Avenues. (Both, Gholston Collection.)

The Brown Hotel became the Sargent Hotel in 1906. The Oregon League for Public Ownership of Railways had offices there in 1907, the same year that the new Portland Automobile Club hosted a free dinner for each of the 150 people in Portland who owned automobiles. For decades, the Sargent Hotel was a place to come together for collective agitation. Meetings were held there in support of east side improvements, including bridges, parks, and fire hydrants. It stood until 1957, and its demise in chronicled in chapter three. (Gholston Collection.)

Brothers Albert C. and Elmer A. Erickson operated this poolroom at 405 Hawthorne Avenue (between Grand and Sixth Avenues) around 1910. Albert also worked as a carman for the Portland Railway, Light & Power Company. The brothers lived nearby at 382 ½ Hawthorne Avenue. They were not related to August Erickson whose saloon on West Burnside Street boasted a bar that was 684 feet long. (Oregon Historical Society, CN 021066.)

This 1910 image shows workers on the nearly completed Hawthorne Avenue Bridge. Portland voters approved $450,000 in bonds in 1907 to replace the failing Madison Bridge, but lawsuits and conflicts with the streetcar company delayed construction (City of Portland Archives, A2004-002.)

In this photograph, the lift span for the new Hawthorne Avenue Bridge waits to be raised into place. It was built on scaffolding, or "falsework," on the east bank of the river just north of Hawthorne Avenue. The rest of the bridge and its towers were all built before the lift span was installed. On November 27, 1910, tugboats towed it into place with the barges underneath it partially submerged. When it was properly positioned, water was pumped from the barges, and the span rose into position. It opened to the public on December 20, 1910. (Gholston Collection.)

After the asylum burned, the grounds around it became Hawthorne Park, which was open to the public but owned by the Hawthorne estate. It was praised as one of the most beautiful places in the city with huge trees and clear water from the spring. Gatherings at the park included large reunions of soldiers and meetings of fraternal organizations, like the Ancient Order of Workman. Concerts and church picnics were held there, and on Sunday nights in the summer, the local churches on the east side organized joint outdoor services for their congregations. The Twenty Sixth Artillery Battalion that trained at Fort Vancouver would sometimes camp overnight in Hawthorne Park when they were on training maneuvers. (City of Portland Archives, A2012-012,1895.)

In 1901, local citizens and booster clubs lobbied the city to purchase the property from the Hawthorne estate for use as a public park. This might have been the first environmental movement in Southeast Portland, and it was not successful. John Charles Olmstead developed a parks plan for Portland in 1904, and it did not include Hawthorne Park. Efforts to gain public ownership of the park continued until 1909, when the Hawthorne estate filled the property with dredge spoils and sold the lots for development. (Oregon Historical Society, OrHi 92633.)

Lewis Randolf Dawson is shown delivering firewood on a horse-drawn cart in 1917 for Hawthorne Fuel. In 1918, the fuel company rented out its horse barn at Ninth Avenue and Hawthorne Avenue and began using delivery trucks. Note the shallow mud, which was probably over some kind of paving. The Heiler block is visible in the background. Located on the southeast corner of Grand and Hawthorne Avenues, it was a three-story building with housekeeping rooms. A street sign next to a horse's ear identifies Sixth Avenue. (Oregon Historical Society, OrgLot1090.)

Damascus creamery bought the Faith Gospel Home at Seventh and Hawthorne Avenues and expanded it into a large dairy distribution center in 1909. Delivery drivers pose with their wagons and horses before heading out to the front porches. (Gholston Collection.)

This is a view of the intersection of Twentieth and Hawthorne Avenues in 1926. The Murrymead Pharmacy is on the corner, and the Hawthorne Sweet Shop is next door. The Hawthorne Theater is showing *Wet Paint* with Raymond Griffith, and a poster on the wall of the pharmacy advertises an upcoming film, *The Grand Duchess and the Waiter* with Adolphe Menjou. (Oregon Historical Society, OrHi 54371.)

The Hawthorne Grocery opened in 1912 at 1101 SE Hawthorne Avenue on the corner of Thirty-seventh Avenue. In 1926, the Bagdad Theater opened across the street. In this image, fresh plums are for sale in the lower-right corner, and boxes of Jell-O are on the shelf in the upper left. The top shelf on the far wall is stocked with breakfast cereal. (Gholston Collection.)

This view is looking east up Hawthorne Avenue from Water Avenue. The building on the left is the Baltimore Hotel. Note the conductors and the passenger awaiting the imminent arrival of the streetcar. This would have been the last stop before the bridge. (Oregon Historical Society, bb013536.)

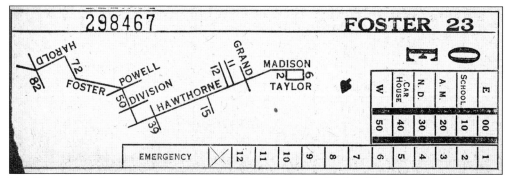

No. 23 was one of several lines that crossed the Hawthorne Bridge. This route turned right at Fiftieth Avenue (the base of Mount Tabor) and went south to connect with Foster Road where it proceeded to the Lents neighborhood. (Gholston Collection.)

Motorman and conductor pose in front of a Portland Railway, Light & Power (PRL&P) Hawthorne Avenue streetcar No. 725 in 1920. The fare was 5¢. The PRL&P was a holding company, financed by Eastern banking interests. According to historian E. Kimbark MacColl in his book *Merchants, Money and Power*, "The monopoly comprised 19 companies in control of 161 miles of railway, 431 passenger cars, and six power plants," and demonstrated "arrogance toward public authority." (City of Portland Archives, A2011-007.16.)

Early Sanborn fire insurance maps show that Hawthorne Avenue between First and Third Avenues was "Planked on Piles 20" and that the railroad along Second Avenue was on a 25-foot-high trestle. The planks and the trestles came down when the low ground was filled. This 1932 image shows the removal of the "bents," which supported the trestle. (City of Portland Archives, A2000-025.285.)

In 1911, George McCroskey started advertising for "2 men to learn automobile repairing and driving" at his Hawthorne Garage. In 1916, when this photograph was taken, Hawthorne Automobile School was advertised as "Oregon's oldest, best equipped, and most practical school." McCroskey also operated Mount Hood Auto Stage from the same location with three departures daily to the village of Government Camp. (Oregon Historical Society, CN 020335.)

This building, at Thirteenth and Hawthorne Avenues, was the location of Francis Motor Car Exchange in 1914. After receiving the Ford franchise, Francis Motor Car Company constructed a new three-story building at Grand and Hawthorne Avenues and moved there in 1920. MBI Motors, servicing Mercedes Benz automobiles, moved into the building in 1973. The new Francis Ford Building is in chapter six. H.N. Mathiesen built his first garage at Seventh and Hawthorne Avenues in 1910. (City of Portland Archives, A2011-014-388.)

Shown here is the Francis Ford paint shop on the second floor of the dealership at the corner of Hawthorne and Grand Avenues. Note the supervisor in the white smock and tie. (Oregon Historical Society, OrHi 6132.)

L.Y. Billingsly (right) confers with sales manager Tom Spencer (left) near his auto showroom on the northwest corner of Seventh Avenue and Hawthorne Boulevard in this 1937 image. The blocks extending north and east from Grand and Hawthorne Avenues came to be known as "Auto Row." (Oregon Historical Society, OrHi 103515.)

In 1905, architects Whidden and Lewis designed a three-story mansion for Phillip Buehner at Fifty-fifth and Hawthorne Avenues, the site of the Perry Prettyman House. Buehner had purchased the Prettyman property in 1890 and had extensively remodeled it using wood he had imported for that purpose. When it was discovered that the wood used for remodeling was full of termites, the building was burned to the ground. (Oregon Historical Society, OrHi 65604.)

The Buehner house is in the distance, and there is land for sale below it in this February 1941 image from the *Oregon Journal*. In the foreground, the streetcar tracks curve from Hawthorne Avenue to Fiftieth Avenue while folks wait on the corner for its arrival. (Photograph courtesy of the *Oregonian*; Oregon Historical Society, 006664.)

This photograph from the 1940s shows the third-floor ballroom of the Buehner house. Buehner came to Oregon in 1887, and he helped to design the Bull Run pipeline for Portland's water system and was a partner in Wolff, Zwicker & Buehner, an important industrial company at the other end of the boulevard. After his experience with the termites, Buehner got into the lumber business. (Western Seminary.)

An upstairs hallway in the Buhner house is shown here. In 1948, the home and surrounding acreage were purchased by Western Seminary. The property is in the National Register of Historic Places. (Western Seminary.)

General Heating employees display the tools of their trade at Ninth and Hawthorne Avenues in 1924. A large furnace, known as an "octopus," is visible through the window. Behind them is Red Men Hall, the Wigwam of Willamette Tribe No. 6 of the Improved Order of the Red Men. In the 1920s, the building hosted dances and meetings of the Brotherhood of American Yeomen, National Association of Letter Carriers, the Order of Scottish Clans, and other groups. In this photograph, a dentist's office is on the second floor, and the ornamentation on the building shows an image associated with the order. The Helium Comedy Club opened upstairs in 2010. (Oregon Historical Society, CN 024387.)

Kaseah Tribe No. 39 of Oswego, Oregon, was a neighboring tribe to Willamette Tribe No. 6. The leader of each tribe is called the sachem. He is assisted by the senior and junior sagamore, the collector of wampum, the prophet, and others. Women may join the Degree of Pocahontas where the leader holds the title of Pocahontas. (Gholston Collection.)

The Improved Order of Red Men traces its roots to the Sons of Liberty, who disguised themselves as Mohawk warriors on the evening of December 16, 1773, boarded the ships of the East India Company, and tossed tea overboard into Boston Harbor to protest British taxes. The original Order of Red Men met in taverns and developed a bad reputation. The improved order was founded around 1835 in Baltimore. In the mid-1920s, it had more than half a million members. In 1991, the order adopted Alzheimer research as its national charity. (Gholston Collection.)

In this aerial photograph, Hawthorne Avenue at SE Fifteenth Avenue is at the left, and its path eastward is indicated by dots in the image. South of the dots, most of the lots in Ladd's Addition are still vacant. The areas north of Hawthorne Avenue already have some dense development, but the areas south, including what came to be known as Colonial Heights, are still largely vacant. The large Buehner house at SE Twenty-sixth Avenue is visible, and it is surrounded by trees. Much of the area around it had been cleared for agriculture. (Oregon Historical Society, bb 000871.)

This 1938 view of traffic on Hawthorne Boulevard crossing Union Avenue eastbound shows rubber-tired trolleys. A radiator shop, a sheet metal shop, a plumbing business, and a dry cleaner can be seen across the street. This block will appear again at the end of the next chapter. (City of Portland Archive, A2005-001.283.)

When the Bagdad Theater opened in 1927, it was the largest theater in Portland outside of downtown. Universal Pictures provided funding to construct a unique Mission/Spanish Colonial Revival–style building with a red tile roof, cast-iron balconettes, and elaborate frescoes. Designed by Thomas and Mercier architects, it is in the National Register of Historic Places. Universal Pictures sent a life-size camel, which had been used as a prop in more than a dozen movies, to enhance the theater's atmosphere. (Photograph courtesy of the *Oregonian*; Oregon Historical Society, OrHi 45753.)

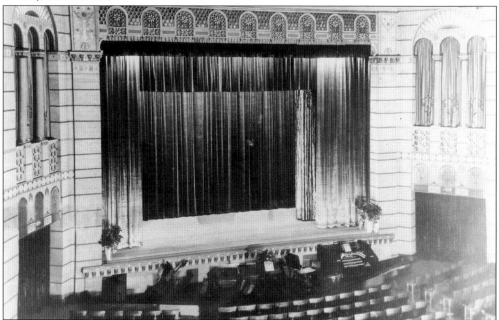

The orchestra pit, complete with instruments, is shown above. Early in its life showing silent pictures, live music was a regular feature. The original auditorium had room for 1,500. In 1973, a wall was built at the front of the balcony, creating a second auditorium upstairs. In 1991, Mike and Brian McMenamin added it to their collection of historic buildings. They removed the wall to create a single auditorium and then removed every other row of seats and installed tables to create space for 590 patrons to enjoy beer and pizza along with their movies. (McMenamins.)

For the first 20 years of its life, the Bagdad was home to both screen and stage performances as well as community events. The opening night advertisement, pictured above, promises orchestral and organ music, singing and dancing, a movie, and "Marilyn Mills with her famous horse Beverly, in person." Later, *One Flew Over the Cuckoo's Nest* had its premiere there in 1975 with star Jack Nicholson in attendance. The movie comes from a novel by Ken Kesey inspired by his experience working at the mental hospital in Salem, Oregon, that replaced Dr. Hawthorne's asylum. (McMenamins.)

The Bagdad's sign going across Hawthorne is visible in this view looking west from the vicinity of Fortieth Avenue. On the right side of the street, Currie's Drugstore can be seen on the corner of Thirty-ninth Avenue, next to the traffic signal. There is a gas station diagonally across, but only a sliver of the sign is visible. There are several large trees on the north side of the street. (Oregon Historical Society, PGE130-74B.)

Three

MID-CENTURY
HAWTHORNE BOULEVARD

Two locally iconic institutions, the Portland Rose Festival and the Fred Meyer store chain, are key characters in this part of the Hawthorne Boulevard story.

Each spring, local high schools across Portland choose princesses who compete to be the Rose Festival queen and preside over the Grand Floral Parade and a festival with rose shows, a carnival, and more. The people in the upcoming images wearing white suits are royal rosarians, the custodians of the tradition and the humans who make it happen. In the flood of 1948, Rose Festival leaders moved their parade from downtown to the east side on short notice. Big crowds watched it in the rain on Hawthorne Boulevard.

Somewhat more modest parades were organized around this time by the Hawthorne Boosters. They paraded in the snow for the March of Dimes, they paraded under the lights to help pass a streetlighting bond, and they paraded from the river to the new Fred Meyer store on the occasion of its grand opening. The Hawthorne Boosters were the mid-century manifestation of merchants organizing, following after the Eastside Commercial Club, the Hawthorne Push Club, and the Hawthorne Merchants Association. Boosters put on drag shows at the Bagdad Theater, and they had men's corset races at their annual picnics.

Fred Meyer was a legendary retailer who had 68 stores in four states at the time of his death in 1978. He had a small Hawthorne Boulevard store briefly in the 1930s. He put his bakery on the site of Hawthorne Springs between Eleventh and Twelfth Avenues and made candy and ice cream there as well. In 1951, Meyer built a one-stop shopping center at the corner of Thirty-ninth Avenue and Hawthorne Boulevard. The pictures from the Fred Meyer Collection open a window on mid-century life on Hawthorne.

The chapter concludes with the construction, in 1957, of ramps to carry Hawthorne Boulevard Bridge traffic directly to Grand Avenue. The five-story hotel from chapters two and three is leveled. The wide stretch of Hawthorne leading down to the river (see the Elks parade on the cover) disappears from view. But driving time from downtown to Southeast Portland is reduced, and motorists do not have to wait at the train crossing.

The Evelle Gift shop is pictured here in 1932 when it had the address of 658 Hawthorne Avenue. The next year, the address of this shop was 1740 SE Hawthorne Boulevard after the city's renumbering. In addition to the variety of items displayed in the windows, Evelle advertised brassware, including novelty ashtrays, dinner bells, and nut crackers. Federal Bakery was next door going east, and the Piggly Wiggly grocery store was on the corner. (City of Portland Archives, A2008-001.102.)

This 1931 image shows Hawthorne Avenue from Twelfth Avenue up the hill to Twentieth Avenue with Cohn Brothers Furniture Store on the right. A streetcar is approaching on Hawthorne Avenue, and the Union Gasoline station is on the right. Several generations of Cohn brothers sold furniture in Spokane, Portland, and throughout Oregon beginning in 1895. (Oregon Historical Society, PGE130-78A.)

Fred Meyer, pictured at right, hands over a check to C.E. Francis for the purchase of a 1932 Ford Crown Victoria. The Francis Ford dealership was at the corner of Grand and Hawthorne Avenues; the story of that building is in chapter six. The car was manufactured at the Portland Ford factory, located nearby at Eleventh Avenue and Division Street. (Oregon Historical Society, OrHi 56380.)

By 1936, the automobile was winning, and the streetcars were in trouble, so the tracks were being pulled out to make the streets smoother. The federal Works Progress Administration (WPA) funded local public works projects to provide jobs for unemployed people during the Depression. In this image, WPA workers are removing the tracks at Fiftieth Avenue and Hawthorne Boulevard while neighborhood youth watch from the sidewalk. Mount Tabor and the historic Buehner mansion are in the background. (City of Portland Archives, A2005-005.1504.18.)

This is a 1936 image of the Shell gasoline station on the southeast corner of Hawthorne Boulevard and Thirty-ninth Avenue. Note the shell-shaped Shell signs atop the gas pumps. The Sunnyside Masonic Lodge is in the background. When it was built in 1919, most of the neighboring properties were residential. (Gholston Collection.)

One attendant cleans the windshield while another collects from the driver. In the background, the Curry Pharmacy is at the northwest corner of the intersection. Fred Curry, the pharmacist, and his wife, Nell, lived just two blocks away on Thirty-eighth Avenue. In 1952, the drugstore building was demolished and removed in a single day to make way for the new Fred Meyer store. (Gholston Collection.)

An attendant checks and refills fluids on a customer's vehicle. This was a common practice in the 20th century. (Gholston Collection.)

The first Fred Meyer retail location on Hawthorne Boulevard was opened in 1938 in the Charles Piper Building at the corner of Thirty-Sixth Avenue. Built in 1929 by F.P. Carson in the Mediterranean style, the building is faced with brick and has parapets with red tile hoods. Originally a Safeway store, it is in the National Register of Historical Places as an example of auto-era commercial development. (Oregon Historical Society, CN 005936.)

A portion of the store's interior is shown here with canned goods lining the shelves. Meyer had opened a large market in the Hollywood neighborhood a few years earlier that could carry many more product lines, and he saw large marketplaces as the future of retailing. This store was too small for that, and he closed it in 1941. (Oregon Historical Society, Coll 199 B32 F2.)

City workers repaint the crosswalk markings in 1939 in the 4900 Block of Hawthorne Boulevard. Achillo Cipolla's Shoe Repair, Joy the Tailor, Alfred Lawton's barbershop, Cleveland's beauty parlor, and Floretta Dry Goods store line the north side. The Safeway store was across the street. (City of Portland Archives, A2005-001.1165.)

By 1935, Safeway had left the store at Thirty-Sixth Avenue and opened this one at Forty-ninth Avenue and another in a triangular building at Twentieth Avenue. Later in this chapter, the Safeway at Fourteenth Avenue is seen at the end of the Grand Floral Parade route. A Portland entrepreneur was behind the rapid growth of the Safeway brand. Marion Barton Skaggs was operating 428 Skaggs stores from his headquarters in Portland when he merged with California-based Safeway (311 stores) and moved to Oakland to be chief executive officer of the combined company. (Photograph courtesy of the *Oregonian*; Oregon Historical Society, 007705.)

A week of Easter festivities sponsored by the Hawthorne Commercial Club kicked off April 3, 1939, with twice daily appearances of Big Bunny at the festival center at Thirty-eighth Avenue and Hawthorne Boulevard. Crystal Market and Grocery at 5012–18 Hawthorne won first place in the window decoration competition, and Valencia Grocery at 1413 Hawthorne was second. On Saturday, Mayor Joseph Carson crowned the festival queen, and there was a pet and floral parade and a Lilliputian circus. (Oregon Historical Society, OrHi 77575.)

In February 1937, Fred Meyer signed a contract to remodel the Liberty Laundry and to add a new building on the lot bounded by Eleventh and Twelfth Avenues, Madison Street, and Hawthorne Boulevard. While most of the facility would be used for baking, he also moved the production operations of candy and ice cream there. (Oregon Historical Society, bb012832.)

Fred Meyer had a grand opening for his new bakery complex in 1939. Visitors got to sample products and learn how their bread was made. Note that Meyer promoted his connection with regional food producers and suppliers. (Oregon Historical Society, Coll199 B10 F7.)

The idea of home-delivered baked goods originated on the East Coast, and Fred Meyer was not the first one to provide this service in Oregon. Note that the independent distributors who did this work had a variety of trucks. (Both, Oregon Historical Society, Coll199 B10 F7 and bb012756.)

In this image, workers pack Valentine candy boxes on a rotating table. Eva Meyer had presided over a small candy kitchen downtown, but in 1936, the Meyers bought the equipment of the Vogan Candy Company, which had gone out of business, and used it to expand production. In his book *My-te-Fine Merchant*, author Fred Leeson relates a story from a longtime employee about the company's candy operation. The manager mentioned to Meyer that they made little if any profit from their Fifth Avenue Candy. Meyer replied, "But Mrs. Meyer likes candy and she likes the candy kitchen." (Oregon Historical Society, bb012834.)

The Rugroden family moved from Minnesota to Hawthorne Boulevard in 1941 for health reasons. Norman Ole Rugroden had heart problems. He is pictured here with his wife, Violet Ruth Rugroden, and their children Cordelle "Corky" Anthony Rugroden and Marlyce Arlene Rugroden. They moved in with Violet's sister and brother-in law in quarters behind the store. Later, for many years, they operated a grocery on the west side at Eleventh Avenue and SW Hall Street. (Gholston Collection.)

Marlyce and Corky perform on the sidewalk. Marlyce was the mother of Norm Gholston, a local historian and image collector. (Gholston Collection.)

The Rugrodens' grocery store was at the corner of Fiftieth Avenue. Norman Rugroden also worked as a carpenter and helped to build the wartime housing complex at Vanport. In the background, Johnny's Valet Service is across the street with a dental office upstairs. A city bus is seen. (Gholston Collection.)

Corky Rugroden sells newspapers at the corner. A Texaco gas station and the Franklin Garage are across the street. (Gholston Collection.)

Beginning in 1935, the Hawthorne Boulevard shops of Portland General Electric (PGE) at the corner of Water Avenue housed repair and maintenance functions for the local utility. Vehicles were repaired and painted. Electrical equipment, including transformers, was also serviced. In 2013, work began to clean up contaminated soil and tanks, and in 2015, the remodeled building became home to a software firm. Pictured here are PGE workers in 1939. (Oregon Historical Society, bb009767.)

Members of the East Side Commercial Club pose after a burlesque performance, which may have included a "womanless fashion show," in this undated *Oregon Journal* photograph. The performance seems to be in an arena. Cultural antecedents of future merchant antics on Hawthorne Boulevard may be found here. (Photograph courtesy of the *Oregonian*; Oregon Historical Society 372A0831.)

In this 1945 aerial photograph, the Hawthorne Boulevard Bridge is at the bottom of the image, and Holman's Transfer is the first building on the right. Two blocks up the street, the PGE Hawthorne Boulevard shops at Water Avenue can be seen with train cars just to the right of them. Proceeding up Hawthorne Boulevard, the six-story Sargent Hotel can be seen, and just past is the Francis Ford dealership with cars on the roof. The diagonal streets of Ladd's Addition intersect Hawthorne Boulevard first at Twelfth Avenue and again at Twentieth Avenue. The spot with trees near the top of the image is the Holman Funeral Home property. (Oregon Historical Society, Album 534, 55027.)

The USS *Rabaul* is shown passing under the Hawthorne Boulevard Bridge in 1946 after completion at the Commercial Ironworks yard. Columbia Ironworks was a longtime Southeast Portland company that expanded rapidly to meet wartime needs. USS *Rabaul* was an escort carrier delivered to the Navy on August 30, 1946, and was never commissioned due to the war's end. It was listed as a reserve until 1972, when it was sold for scrap. While waiting to be scrapped, it was used as the setting for the final scenes of the 1973 Clint Eastwood movie *Magnum Force*. (Oregon Historical Society, PF2173.)

Roadwork is in progress on lower Hawthorne Boulevard in this image. The railroad crossing with lights and tower is in view on the right. In the center of the image at the top of the hill, the Francis Ford sign is visible. On the south side of Hawthorne Boulevard, the Dennis Uniform factory is visible. The company moved to 105 Hawthorne Boulevard in 1950 and stayed there when the bridge ramps were constructed in front of its building. It celebrated its 100th anniversary as a Portland business in 2020. (Gholston Collection.)

Portlanders stack sandbags to keep floodwaters out of J&H Grain on the corner of Hawthorne Boulevard and Water Avenue during the 1948 flood. Louis Schwab's machine shop is next to J&H. The two-story building in the distance is the Eastside Terminal. While large-scale filling operations early in the 20th century raised inner Southeast Portland above typical high water, in major flood events, many lower blocks can be inundated. (City of Portland Archives, A2005-001.1165.)

The 1948 flood wiped out Vanport, a wartime housing development in North Portland. Vanport was built during World War II by industrialist Henry Kaiser to house the workers in his shipyards. On Memorial Day, the Columbia River breached the dike that protected the low-lying community. The 18,500 residents had just 35 minutes to flee the rising waters. Fifteen Vanport residents died. In this photograph, onlookers view the flood devastation, and people are gathered on a roof. (Oregon Historical Society, OrgLot131-004.)

The flooding and the loss of life led many, including Mayor Earl Riles, to call for cancelling the traditional Grand Floral Parade, the largest event of the annual Portland Rose Festival. However, association leaders maintained that more than $23,000 would be lost if the festival was called off. With less than a week to go, a compromise was reached, and the parade was moved from its traditional downtown route to the east side. Although Vanport no longer existed, its float, pictured above, won second place in its division. (Gholston Collection.)

Barbara Logue was the 1948 Rose Festival princess from Washington High School, and she was chosen from among the other princesses to be the queen. Thus the Washington High School band marched in front of her float (pictured above), just behind the Marine color guard that led the parade. Washington High was the school that Nobel Laureate Linus Pauling left in 1916 and graduated from in 1982. That story is told in chapter six. (Gholston Collection.)

The parade started on Foster Road in Lents and came north on Fiftieth Avenue to Hawthorne Boulevard. This picture shows the crowd waiting at Fourteenth Avenue and Hawthorne Boulevard where the parade would disband. The queen's float can be seen in the distance near the top of the hill. Note the mid-century Safeway location. (Oregon Historical Society, OrHi 95070.)

S.E. 36th AND HAWTHORNE - PORTLAND,

The Bagdad Tavern and Marigold Chop Suey are in the foreground on the left. On the right, Lets Go Inn, Hawthorne Dry Goods, and Bagdad Drugs are located in the historic Francis Building. The Francis was the first masonry building in this area, which was mostly residential.

The entrance for the moving and storage company between the dry goods store and the tavern was the former hallway to the Echo Theater. In the distance on the right, Nick's Coney Island can be seen. (Oregon Historical Society, OrgLot 1275 B2 F11.)

The Hawthorne Boosters' float "Blooming Merry-go-Round," pictured above, won first place in its division in the 1950 Rose Festival Grand Floral Parade. Al Mendleson was president of the boosters that year, and he got credit for the win. Boosters sponsored a basketball team, a March of Dimes drive, a Christmas tree at Thirty-seventh Avenue, and an all-male burlesque review at the Bagdad Theater to raise money for college scholarships. (Photograph courtesy of the *Oregonian*; Oregon Historical Society, Lot 850 B2 F22.)

Durrie's restaurant, on the corner of Twentieth Avenue and Hawthorne Boulevard, is in the center of this 1951 photograph. The Plaza drugstore is across Twentieth Avenue, and an Atlantic Richfield gas station is on the other side of Hawthorne Boulevard. Just past Durrie's is Herner's Radio. This is one of the two five-way intersections on the corner of Ladd's Addition. Elliot Street intersects at a 45-degree angle and runs diagonally across Ladd's Addition to the intersection of Twelfth Avenue and Division Street. (City of Portland Archives, A2005-001.301.)

The boosters' 1952 president, Tony Nizic, is shown here moving the hands of the clock. Former boosters presidents Al Mendleson (left) and Ralph Granato (right) hold the banner. Ott's Radio, Appliance, and Record Store and Nick's Coney Island are across the street. Daylight savings time was controversial in 1952 when Oregon governor Douglas McKay blocked it statewide while Portland and other cities adopted it. Oregon voters made Standard Time mandatory in November of that year through a state ballot initiative. Daylight savings time failed at the ballot in 1954 and 1960 but finally passed in 1962. (Oregon Historical Society, OrHi 74183.)

Three gas stations on the north side of Hawthorne Boulevard can be seen in this view looking west from Twelfth Avenue. A Chevron gas station is on the near corner with a Flying A across Twelfth Avenue and the Texaco at Eleventh Avenue. A Plymouth sign is visible in the distance on the right, and beyond it is the three-story Francis Ford dealership. (Portland City Archives, A2005-001.302.)

This photograph is from the Hawthorne Boosters' 1951 annual picnic that drew 2,000 guests to Viking Park by the Sandy River in Troutdale. Events at the picnic included a Civil War–themed baseball game, pitting merchants from the south side of Hawthorne Boulevard against those from the north; music by the Hawthorne Hotshots; and a mystery corset race. Note that the booster at left in the photograph was apparently dressed for the race. (Photograph by Jean Cross; Oregon Historical Society, Coll 199 B13 F7.)

The Hawthorne Boulevard Fred Meyer store was built in 4 months and 20 days. Meyer claimed that it was a world record for speedy construction. Note that excavations for the new building have started while demolition of previous structures was still in progress. In the background, the Masonic temple, Atlas Gas Station, and the Hawthorne Boulevard Branch of the First National Bank are visible. In the upper left, a tree blooms in April. (Oregon Historical Society, Coll 199 B13 F6.)

Opening day festivities on Tuesday September 11, 1951, kicked off with a motor parade, sponsored by the Hawthorne Boosters; it started at Water Avenue and made its way up the boulevard to Thirty-ninth Avenue. The doors swung open at 2:00 p.m., and the first 10,000 visitors got a piece of the 1,500-pound birthday cake shown here. The grand opening celebration lasted five days and included performances by Norbeck's Mouse Circus, Kordo the human monkey, the Granato amateur talent show, and daily appearances by Mr. Peanut. There was a mammoth food and merchandising exposition and a citywide baking contest. (Oregon Historical Society, Coll 199 B13 F7.)

Children were not forgotten in the festivities. The merry-go-round above was sponsored by the Hawthorne Boosters. On Saturday morning, movies were provided for children at the Bagdad Theater. Saturday afternoon, there was a mutt parade and bench show limited to children with dogs. Through the 1950s, the boosters supported the Junior Rose Parade and the process for selecting its royalty. Each spring, they hosted an event at the Bagdad Theater where fifth grade couples from area elementary schools would compete to be named princess and prince on the Junior Rose Festival Court. (Oregon Historical Society, Coll 199 B13 F7.)

Fred Meyer's one-stop shopping concept was new to the neighborhood. Beyond groceries, the store offered clothing, lawn furniture, baby strollers, fountain pens, radios, and much more, as shown in this photograph. Fred Meyer was a featured speaker at national meetings of retailers, and his methods were copied by chains across the country. The retailer that became Walmart began by using Meyer's methods, according to Leeson's book *My-Te-Fine Merchant*. (Oregon Historical Society, bb012787.)

The new stores had two acres of rooftop parking with space for 300 cars. Meyer claimed it was the largest rooftop parking structure in the world. There was another acre of parking underneath that provided space for many of the grand opening festivities. Over the years, additional store space eliminated the ground-floor parking and took over half of the roof. Also visible in this photograph are a bank, a title insurance company, and a laundry and dry cleaner. (Oregon Historical Society, bb012760.)

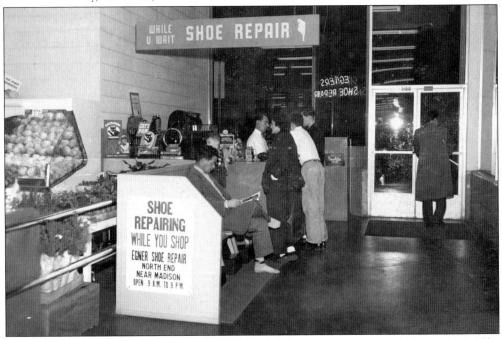

Eventually, the Fred Meyer Shopping Center added a florist, a jeweler, an optician, and a coffee shop. A laundromat and a tiny locksmith building were constructed in the parking lot. Egners offered shoe repair while one shopped or, as pictured here, while one waited in his or her socks. (Oregon Historical Society, Coll 199 B13 F9.)

The Imperial Roller Rink was built in 1925. In 1933, the Unemployed Citizens League sponsored a skating party there to collect canned goods and groceries. The Women's Committee of the American Institute of Banking held a skating party there in 1947. The poster at left advertises 1954 activities, and the image below shows the rink. In 1957, Hawthorne Boulevard Bridge ramp construction placed a busy street just a dozen feet from the second-floor rink. It closed in 1976. (Both, Gholston Collection.)

THE **IMPERIAL** SKATERS

Present

FUN Galore in '54

★ MON. JANUARY 18
3 BIG SHOWS ★ TUES. JANUARY 19
★ WED. JANUARY 20
DOORS OPEN; 7:00 p.m., SHOW 8:15

IMPERIAL ROLLER RINK

419 S. E. MADISON BETWEEN GRAND & UNION

Imperial Roller Rink   Portland, Ore.

Hawthorne Boulevard was the setting for a demonstration of modern streetlighting in October 1954, seen in this *Oregon Journal* photograph. Both fluorescent and mercury vapor lights were temporarily installed in a project jointly undertaken by Portland General Electric and the City of Portland. On October 16, the Jaycees and the Hawthorne Boosters were sponsors of a kickoff parade with bands, antique cars, and fire engines. The demonstration and the parade were aimed at building support for a city tax levy to install streetlighting. A few weeks later, the levy passed. (Photograph courtesy of the *Oregonian*; Oregon Historical Society, OrHi 65410.)

Mail carrier Hughie Motley meets up with Princess and Shiner at the mail storage box at Forty-sixth Avenue and Hawthorne Boulevard, as seen in this 1955 *Oregon Journal* photograph. The dogs accompanied Motley on his route. (Photograph courtesy of the *Oregonian*; Oregon Historical Society, CN 013250.)

In 1957, US armed services partnered with Portland civic groups to cosponsor floats in the Rose Festival Grand Floral Parade. Foster Boosters worked with the Marines, Sellwood Moreland Businessmen's Association paired with the Navy, and the Hawthorne Boosters partnered with the US Air Force on the float "Racing with the Moon," pictured above. (Oregon Historical Society, bb002454.)

Michael and Patti Carulli were the pilots for Hawthorne Boulevard's space program. The float received second place in its division. (Oregon Historical Society, OrgLot 431 B8F1.)

The photograph above looks west in 1956, just before construction of ramps linking Grand Avenue with the bridge over the top of Hawthorne Boulevard. A surplus store was operating from the first floor of the Sargent Hotel, formerly the Brown Hotel. Below is the view of the south side of the same intersection. From left, the Italo Social Club, Hawthorne Smoke Shop, and Joe's Drugs and Fountain are on Grand Avenue. McKenzie Café and the Drift Inn are among the businesses on Hawthorne Boulevard. (Both, Multnomah County Archives.)

The remains of the foundation of the Sargent Hotel are shown here, after its demolition. The businesses on the south side of Hawthorne Boulevard are still operating. From right, an office supply store, IXL barbershop, McKenzie Café, Johnny Tiny Café, Drift Inn, Hawthorne Smoke Shop, and Joe's Drugs and Fountain with dentist Dr. George Votran upstairs are all operating next to the construction zone. (Multnomah County Archives.)

On the street in front of the Drift Inn workers assemble steel reinforcements for the eastern edge of the new Hawthorne Boulevard Bridge ramps. The view down the boulevard from this point will be gone soon. (Multnomah County Archives.)

Looking up the street to McKenzie Café and the Drift Inn, a wall is now in place. The first of the new bridge bents can also be seen with Francis Ford in the background. The office supply store is for rent. (Multnomah County Archives.)

Eight years later, ramps associated with Interstate 5 were built above other ramps that were constructed above Hawthorne Boulevard. In this photograph, giant pillars to carry the freeway overhead dwarf the Hawthorne Boulevard Bridge. (City of Portland Archives, A2004-002.11574.)

Four

HAWTHORNE BOULEVARD REBORN

Hawthorne had a rundown feeling by the late 1960s as urban poverty crept through nearby neighborhoods. But large old homes with cheap rent drew young people, many involved in organizing against war, imperialism, capitalism, and patriarchy. They got to know their older neighbors, some of whom had worked in similar movements in the 1930s. Joining forces, they organized Portland Action Committees Together and, through it, neighborhood associations in Buckman, Sunnyside, Richmond, and Hosford-Abernethy. Activists won funding for antipoverty and infrastructure programs and helped stop a proposed freeway that would have cut the neighborhood in half.

In the 1980s, Hawthorne businesses were regrouping many years after the Hawthorne Boosters ceased operations. Roger Jones from the Sporting House tavern, Mike Morelli from Morelli's Texaco, and a few others convened a meeting in 1983 and created the Hawthorne Boulevard Business Association. They worked to confront the challenging issues of a rundown district, starting a foot patrol to reduce crime on the boulevard and launching an annual street fair. In 1985, the association won a three-year grant from the Main Street Project of the National Trust for Historic Preservation.

In 1992, Rachel Ann Hardyman traced the interaction of business revitalization with cultural influences for her master's thesis in geography, "Hawthorne Boulevard: Commercial Gentrification and the Creation of an Image." Her scholarly research covers the period from 1980 to 1992 on Hawthorne between Twenty-eighth and Thirty-ninth Avenues. In addition to census research and field interviews, she used city directories to find year-to-year changes in the business mix.

For example, she found that there were 10 restaurants in 1980 and 18 in 1992 and that 1 clothing store existed in 1980 and 11 in 1992. She writes, "Three parallel trends can be distinguished in the makeup of the business mix: a shift from services to retailing; a move toward a regional, rather than a neighborhood market area; and a cultural upgrading associated with the influx of increasingly expensive stores." These trends are common in areas that are gentrifying, but Hardyman finds a difference on Hawthorne Boulevard, stating the following: "Gentrification seems to have been (unconsciously) undertaken by an intellectual, rather than an economic, elite."

Two story lines intertwine—communities of people who are empowered and connected with each other and businesses that are smart, creative, and caring. Elements of the Hawthorne Boulevard phenomenon are getting clearer, but others are harder to define.

In the late 1970s, one could meet all kinds of people at La Casa de Rios.

La Casa de Rios bridged the gap from the old Hawthorne Boulevard to the new. It was the kind of place where everybody felt welcome. It started when Elsie Rios sent her son David Martinez to check out the Oregon Trail Burger restaurant. It was closing, and she was looking for a place on Hawthorne Boulevard to start a restaurant. David provided a favorable report, and La Casa de Rios was launched in 1972. (David A. Martinez.)

Elsie Rios and her son Eddie Martinez are pictured above. Elsie was the head cook and the boss. Her son David worked with her in the kitchen, and Eddie handled the public relations. The food was handmade, fresh, and affordably priced. Neighborhood folks without a lot of money could have dinner and a beer and think about being an entrepreneur one day. (Maria Cruz de Lara.)

With the front windows of La Casa de Rios behind her, Gina Martinez brings forks and napkins for diners. On the right of the image, the refrigerator is decorated with photographs of customers and some foreign currency, while a communal sugar dispenser typical of this period can be seen in the foreground. Gina was married to David, and Elsie was her mother-in-law. La Casa was a family restaurant. (Maria Cruz de Lara.)

Michele Lemme takes a break after her shift as a waitress at La Casa de Rios. Note that the chairs are stacked on the tables, and the restaurant is closed. (Maria Cruz de Lara.)

Repairs on the sidewalks on the north side of Hawthorne Boulevard between Thirty-seventh and Thirty-eighth Avenues are seen here in 1971. Beaver Trading Post, pictured at left, opened at 3713 Hawthorne Boulevard in 1968. Bergeson's Coffee Shop was originally located in the Fred Meyer Shopping Center, just one block to the east. Wayne Stookey Jewelers, Terry's Dress Shop, and the House of Linoleum are also visible. Across the street, the First National Bank and the Masonic temple can be seen. (City of Portland Archives, A2012-005, 1971.)

When the Safeway store at Twenty-eighth Avenue opened in 1963, there was a large parking lot between the store and the street, as seen in the image above. In the 1980s, the store was open 24 hours a day. When Safeway built a new, larger store on the same lot in 2011, zoning regulations required better pedestrian access. The new store opened directly to the sidewalk, and most of the parking was underground. (Hawthorne Boulevard Business Association.)

The Beaver Building, pictured above, appeared in chapter two as Red Men Hall. The heads of Indian chiefs are still visible as ornaments in the building facade. In this 1981 photograph, the showroom windows on the corner of the first floor have been covered, and tenants include a social service agency. Times were hard, and many buildings were vacant. (City of Portland Archives, A2012-008.523.6.)

The Charles Pope Building, previously home to Safeway and Fred Meyer and now listed in the National Register of Historic Places, was a boarded-up warehouse in 1982. Note that the brickwork under the windows does not match the rest of the building because that space was open to the street when groceries were sold there. Union Furniture had a total of 10 storefronts on Hawthorne Boulevard, many of which were used for storage. This was a low point for the historic buildings on Hawthorne Boulevard, but change was on the way. (City of Portland Archives, A2012-008.795.12.)

Mike Morelli opened his first service station in 1950 on the corner of Fifty-first Avenue and Hawthorne Boulevard. In 1964, he moved to Forty-fifth Avenue and Hawthorne Boulevard and, later, to the pictured location near Fortieth Avenue. After the closure of this station, the only Hawthorne gas station was at Twelfth Avenue. (Hawthorne Boulevard Business Association.)

In 1987, Jack Herer opened the Third Eye, a counterculture landmark located right next door to Morelli's service station on Hawthorne Boulevard. The first floor featured posters, jewelry, and tie-dyed clothing. Up the stairs (adults only) was a head shop with pipes, rolling papers, and stash containers disguised as common household objects. Jack was an internationally recognized cannabis expert, and the Jack Herer Cup is awarded each year to recognize cannabis excellence. His son Mark took over in 2001, but legalization hurt head shops as paraphernalia purchases shifted to the new cannabis stores, and it closed in 2017. (Hawthorne Boulevard Business Association.)

When Cinnamon Chaser opened Presents of Mind at 3633 Hawthorne Boulevard in 1989, there were no stores that carried the cards and gifts that she wanted to buy. She built an inventory that emphasized locally made and environmentally friendly products. Beautiful jewelry crafted by local artists is across the room from weird wind-up toys, and half the store is dedicated to selling cards. The concept was perfect for Hawthorne Boulevard. Neighborhood people became loyal customers, and people from all over came to see what was happening. (Cinnamon Chaser.)

Ben Davis opened Grand Central Baking's first Portland location at Twenty-second Avenue and Hawthorne Boulevard in 1993. His mother, Gwenyth Bassetti, started the company in Seattle in 1989, and her rustic Italian breads gained nationwide acclaim. In the image above, Ben is in the center of the group at right peering into the old Dragonfly Garden's store that would soon be the new Grand Central. It is a certified-B corporation and thus is committed to prioritize social and environmental concerns alongside profitability. (Grand Central.)

Karen Harding was running a pioneering espresso cart at Portland State University when the owner of the Sunnyside Up Bakery and Café recruited her to take over the restaurant. Thus, in 1988, she created the Cup & Saucer Café in the heart of Hawthorne. She recalls that "many good and kind and varied folks gave that street a wonderful, homey and accepting feel." In this image, she is preparing cookies. In 1992, Rachel Hardyman did field research for her master's thesis at the Cup & Saucer Café. She reports the following: "Among its diverse clientele are a large number of lesbians who regularly outnumber everyone else in the restaurant. Its reputation is reinforced, and its clientele confirmed, by the numerous flyers pinned up outside: Lesbian Pride Dance, The Other Queen's Ball." Later, she notes, "This restaurant exudes political correctness—there is no ice in the water, no judgements made about clients, and no tolerance of bigotry." (Karen Harding.)

Karen Harding, with Adam, an employee, looks through the front window of the café on the occasion of the café's first anniversary. Harding remembers that Hawthorne Boulevard was "rough" and more political in 1988. A poster in the background promotes an upcoming performance by Ranch Romance, "the Northwest's finest She Buckaroo band," with special guest Tret Fure, an important musician and producer in the women's music movement. There are also fliers for a massage therapist, a bulimia support group, and a multimedia concert at the nearby Echo Theater. (Karen Harding.)

Karen Harding, Matt Ethridge, and Stephanie (last name unknown) are serving the people at the front counter of the Cup & Saucer. The many business cards and handwritten notes on the overflowing bulletin board suggest a community that is in touch with itself. One of the flyers advertises the REACH Paint-A-Thon. REACH (Recreation, Education, Access, Commerce, and Housing) was founded in 1982 as a neighborhood community development corporation, and its annual paint-a-thon is a volunteer effort to fix up the homes of seniors and low-income folks in the neighborhood. (Karen Harding.)

Members of the Hawthorne Boulevard Business Association (HBBA) gather to announce their sixth annual street fair in 1989. Mike Morelli loaned the car, and Harlequin Costumes provided the duds. From left to right are Roger Jones, Sporting House Pub; Judy Thompson, Liberty Group Realtors; HBBA president Mick Chase, Hospitality Graphics; Doris Glasser, Hawthorne Coffee Merchant; Barbara Jones, Hawthorne Liquor Store; Linda Molatore, US Bank; HBBA National Main Street manager Rob DeGraff; Nannette Taylor, Columbia Theater Company; Judy Thompson's daughter Mia Thompson; Diane Trapp, Illusionary Design; and a "Joe Coffee" sales person at the Coffee Merchant. Rob DeGraff was hired as the Main Street manager and tasked with improving communication, recruiting new businesses, and helping connect those businesses to vacant property. A report at the end of the project found a net gain for the boulevard of 32 businesses and 75 jobs between September 1985 and June 1988. (Photograph by David Wilds; Hawthorne Boulevard Business Association.)

The Hawthorne Boulevard transition incudes the departure of the Adult Center porn store and the arrival of the women's clothing boutique El Mundo and the Hawthorne Coffee Merchant (sign on the sidewalk), as seen here in this 1987 image. El Mundo and the Hawthorne Coffee Merchant were in the historic 1909 Sensel Grocery Store Building, which is in the National Register of Historic Places. It is one of the few surviving wood frame streetcar-era commercial buildings. (Hawthorne Boulevard Business Association.)

Across the street, Don Juan's Restaurant and Lounge is next door to Macheesmo Mouse. Don Juan's was a traditional restaurant that had a problem with some shootings in its parking lot. Macheesmo was a small local chain, founded by Tiger Warren in 1981; it was a pioneer in healthy fast food. Neighborhood residents fondly remember Macheesmo's "Cactus Cooler" beverage. The chain had grown to 10 stores by 1999, when Warren and his three sons died tragically in a floatplane crash on the Columbia River. (Hawthorne Boulevard Business Association.)

In 1980, Don Oman and Peter DeGarmo were both progressive activists with the Sunnyside Chapter of Oregon Fair Share. They were largely responsible for securing a 70-percent favorable vote in two precincts for a People's Utility District to replace investor-owned utilities with a democratically controlled electric district. In 1983, Don and Peter opened Pastaworks, featuring fresh pasta, imported groceries, and a good bottle of wine at a decent price. They were radicals, and they became entrepreneurs that changed Hawthorne Boulevard. Pictured is HBBA staff Rob Degraff (right) and others in front of the store. (Hawthorne Boulevard Business Association.)

Jack and Iva Elmer started making candy and cakes at 4733 Hawthorne Boulevard in 1986, and their creations have won international awards. In this photograph are, from left to right, Rob DeGraff, staff for the Main Street Project; an unidentified woman, Jack Elmer, and Iva Elmer. (City of Portland Archives, A2010-003.)

Hawthorne Boulevard's connection with the legendary band the Grateful Dead is nowhere clearer than it is at the Barley Mill Pub. Owners Mike and Brian McMenamin are longtime fans, and the Barley Mill is packed with art and memorabilia connected to the band. The Barley Mill opened in 1983, shortly before brewpubs were legal. In 1985, the brothers opened the Hillsdale Brewery and Public House, and they have continued to expand with more than 60 locations in Oregon and Washington. The Barley Mill is their oldest pub. In the image above, the banner says, "A Neighborhood Place for Family and Friends." (McMenamins.)

This view of Hawthorne Boulevard from the roof of the Fred Meyer store comes from the Portland Development Commission's reconnaissance of the neighborhood in anticipation of some kind of development assistance. Beaver Books is on the right, and the sign for the carpet store can be seen beyond it. The Tu-Be Tavern sign is visible in the distance on the left. (City of Portland Archives, A2010-003.)

Renowned mandolinist and instrument collector David Grisman tries out a Koa Kumalae ukulele at Artichoke Music in this photograph. Grisman's broad range fits well with the diverse musical interests of Hawthorne Boulevard cultures. A virtuoso in bluegrass and jazz, he plays on two songs on the Grateful Dead's *American Beauty* album ("Ripple" and "Friend of the Devil"). Grisman was part of the band Old and in the Way with the Grateful Dead's Jerry Garcia and Vassar Clements, a fiddler who played in Bill Monroe's band and with other bluegrass legends. (Artichoke Music.)

Felim Egan on Irish button accordion and Bob Soper on fiddle perform in front of the original Artichoke store near Thirty-fifth Avenue. Steve Einhorn moved Artichoke to Hawthorne Boulevard from NW Twenty-first Avenue in 1983. He recalls that the neighborhood was "very open and friendly" with a "good mix of the old neighborhood businesses and residents with the new 'hipster riff-raff.' " (Artichoke Music.)

Steve Einhorn and Kate Power check progress on Artichoke's second and much larger Hawthorne Boulevard location in 1997. At Thirty-second Avenue, there was room for the store, music classrooms, and a performance space in back. The Backgate Stage hosted performances by musicians across many genres, including Odetta, Dave Van Ronk, and Tom Paxton. (Artichoke Music.)

Andy Sterling demonstrates a hurdy-gurdy to some visiting French-speaking theater folk. In 2007, Steve Einhorn and Kate Power left Artichoke, and it became a nonprofit corporation, managed by a volunteer board. Artichoke left Hawthorne Boulevard in 2017 for a new location on Powell Boulevard. (Artichoke Music.)

Powell's first came to Hawthorne Boulevard in 1987 with its Books for Cooks and Garderners store, located just east of Pastaworks at the site of the old Beaver Bookstore. It opened Hawthorne Boulevard's Powell's in 1992, which is much smaller than its mother ship on West Burnside Street but still requires a map. The photograph above is from the early days of the Hawthorne Boulevard store. (Powell's Books.)

In 1983, the Bread and Ink Café, pictured, began serving upscale eclectic food at moderate prices. Earlier in this chapter, this building was seen as a boarded-up warehouse for Union Furniture. In chapter three, it was a Fred Meyer grocery store. Nearing a century on Hawthorne Boulevard, this building tells the story of the ups and downs of the district. (Hawthorne Boulevard Business Association.)

Five

21ST-CENTURY HAWTHORNE BOULEVARD

How did Hawthorne happen? Part of it is the right geography. In a message to the Hawthorne Boulevard Business Association in 1985, Pres. Roger Jones said, "Thank you Mt. Tabor," and he notes that the "natural geographic boundaries in the drawbridge and the active volcano . . . held back the potential growth of this bridgehead traffic arterial" and saved Hawthorne from the auto-oriented development that happened elsewhere in east Portland.

For many of the merchants in the previous chapter, being in the right place at the right time was an element of their success. It was serendipitous when cheap rent allowed new ideas to take root. It was earned good fortune when grant applications were successful and public funds came to assist revival.

Favorable geography and unexpected business opportunities explain a lot, but cultural and political factors were an essential ingredient. The chorus for a popular anthem of the time concludes as follows: "Everybody get together / try to love one another / right now." As corny as it might seem to 21st-century readers, these were words to live by for many folks on Hawthorne Boulevard.

But there was struggle as well as love. The civil rights movement was fresh, and feminism was rapidly emerging. The foment drove new ways of thinking that helped shape Hawthorne Boulevard.

Has Hawthorne Boulevard gentrified? In the last chapter, Rachel Hardyman's 1992 analysis of gentrification on Hawthorne Boulevard was explored. She explained that the presence of subcultural groups in the Hawthorne community makes it hard to accurately characterize that phenomenon on the boulevard. She says, "Gentrification varies from place to place and the tipping point at which revitalization becomes gentrification depends on individual circumstances."

In the 21st century, Hawthorne Boulevard still has grocery stores that serve the neighborhood, affordable restaurants, and used clothing stores that are intermixed with fine dining establishments and exclusive upscale boutiques. Small contradictions abound.

The Hawthorne Boulevard Business Association still puts on a street fair every August, and after many years of trying, it has permission to close the street to traffic. The street fair still draws a large and diverse crowd.

The new asylum on Hawthorne Boulevard is not a mental hospital but instead a food cart pod. Many old buildings are gone, but there are new sculptures that remember them. Nick's Coney Island has weathered the storms on Hawthorne Boulevard and still serves a great Coney.

A ribbon-cutting reopens the Hawthorne Boulevard Bridge in 1999. It was closed for sidewalk widening and painting, which created more room for pedestrians and cyclists, arrested rust, and changed the color from beige to green. Multnomah County chair Beverly Stein, in the center, wears a Hawthorne Boulevard Bridge T-shirt, Congressman Earl Blumenauer is wearing shorts and holding his bike helmet, and Roger Jones of the Hawthorne Boulevard Business Association is behind Blumenauer. On the right are royal rosarians, and behind the children are, from left to right, former Multnomah County commissioners Lisa Naito, Tanya Collier, and Dianne Linn. Others are unidentified. (Multnomah County Archives.)

In 1968, the Piggly Wiggly grocery store was at this location, and Bobby Kennedy gave a speech here less than two weeks before he was assassinated in California. Later, it was the Daily Grind, a store that specialized in natural foods. In this picture, one can see that the old has passed away, and the New Seasons will come. (Photograph by Owen Scholes.)

Annie Han and Daniel Mihaylo, Seattle artists trained in architecture, received a commission to create sculptures next to the city's new streetcar line in 2013. The artwork is called "Inversion +/-," and it consists of three separate pieces, one of which is pictured above. Two of the massive metal installations are at the Hawthorne Boulevard bridgehead on Grand Avenue, and one is at the Morrison Street bridgehead. At the corner of Hawthorne Boulevard and Grand Avenue, at the location where the Brown/Sargent Hotel once stood, a metal plaque explains the following: "The form of the sculpture is derived from several buildings that were demolished as part of 1950's highway construction . . . the sculpture explores the scale and complexity of the lost civic fabric, suggesting an alternate reading of history or a future not yet formed." (Photograph by Richard Melling.)

Food cart pods are a 21st-century phenomena, and there are several on Hawthorne Boulevard. This one is named for Dr. Hawthorne's asylum and features his image. Cheese steak is on the menu for the cart visible through the gears. (Both, photograph by Richard Melling.)

The pod is between Eleventh and Twelfth Avenues on land that was part of the old asylum grounds and later Hawthorne Park. It opened in 2019. (Photograph by Richard Melling.)

Old and new buildings mix in this view from the 38th annual Hawthorne Boulevard Street Fair in 2019. The two-story, brick Douglas Building on the right was constructed in 1929 and is in the National Register of Historic Places. Just to the left, the upper stories of the Hub, built in 2018, are visible. On the left side of the picture is the Peterson Building from 1905, and in the distance (with the sloping roof) the Hawthorne Condominiums, built in 2015, are visible. (Author's collection.)

Musicians play the tuba and saxophone for the street fair crowd. Note that the sax player also plays the drum and has a tambourine on his foot. The salon in the background shows the upscale influences in the neighborhood. Next door is Imeda's Shoes, whose name recalls Imelda Marcos, the first lady of the Philippines for 22 years who reportedly owned 3,000 pairs of shoes. (Author's collection.)

There were already three popular used clothing stores within two blocks when Goodwill opened its Hawthorne Boulevard store. Here, the store has sidewalk sale items for the street fair. The inventory for this store is carefully curated, and prices are competitive with the nearby stores. (Author's collection.)

A guitar-playing Sasquatch with a seagull for a friend welcomes shoppers to a street fair booth in front of the Presents of Mind card shop, a pioneer merchant in the Hawthorne Boulevard revival. In a chapter three photograph, Marigold Chop Suey was on the corner, and the Bagdad Tavern was next door. Later, the wall was removed, and Starbucks now occupies both spaces. (Author's collection.)

Two men staff a booth advocating voluntary human extinction. Hawthorne Boulevard's tolerance for a broad range of social and political views is well known. Powell's Books for Home and Garden is in the background. (Author's collection.)

Nick's Coney Island started in 1932 and continues into the 21st century. Its Coney Island, a hot dog covered in chili, is its signature dish. Founder Nick Carlascio was active in the Hawthorne Boosters. Frank Nudo took over in 1960. He was much loved by his customers and filled the walls of the tavern with autographed pictures of sports celebrities and politicians. In 2008, Nudo retired. In this image, one can see him looking out the front door of the tavern. (Jan Capalener.)

Six

HAWTHORNE BOULEVARD PLACES AND PEOPLE

Some stories do not fit neatly into a chronological organization model. However, they are true and interesting, and they may be particularly helpful in answering the questions posed in the introduction.

This chapter starts with a look at a structure that was constructed as a three-story auto dealership, rebuilt as a six-story office building for a Savings & Loan, and then sold to Multnomah County to be the official seat of county government. The author's interest in this building and its empty elevator shafts grew during his long employment there. The second building under consideration in this chapter started as a mansion for a local capitalist, became a naturopathic sanitarium, and then became a funeral home. Both of these buildings are landmarks that have been recycled for new uses.

Three human beings are spotlighted at the end of this book. Doc Severinsen is familiar to the generation that watched *The Tonight Show Starring Johnny Carson*. For local folks, the tiny building on Hawthorne Boulevard where his father practiced dentistry is a diminutive landmark. The John Reed Bookstore was just a block or two from the dental office. The story of one of its proprietors, Martina Gangle Curl, illustrates some of the ways art and politics connect on Hawthorne Boulevard. The author was privileged to be arrested and tried in Columbia County, Oregon, with Martina Curl in 1976 as part of a protest against the Trojan Nuclear Power Plant.

Linus Pauling gets the last word. He revolutionized chemistry with his discoveries about the way molecules behave, and he won a Nobel Prize for that. But he did not rest on his laurels. He and his wife, Ava, were important leaders in the struggle to limit and abolish nuclear weapons, and he won a Nobel Peace Prize as well. He was the only person to earn two unshared Nobel Prizes in different fields. Readers who have not heard Hawthorne Boulevard's different drummer yet may find the Pauling quotation at the end to be particularly helpful.

Questioning authority, opposing discrimination, supporting creativity, doing well by doing good, and celebrating together are all things that are happening on Hawthorne Boulevard. Visitors find hospitality and unique items from artists in the neighborhood and around the world. Local residents find community.

C.E. Francis started with a used car dealership on Hawthorne Boulevard in 1912. In 1914, he became an authorized Ford dealer, and in 1916, he moved from Thirteenth and Hawthorne Avenues to a new three-story building at the corner of Grand Avenue. The ground floor had a large showroom on the Hawthorne Avenue side and a service department with a driveway out to Grand Avenue. The second floor had paint and repair shops, and the third floor was storage. (Oregon Historical Society, OrHi 72063.)

Francis Ford was a landmark and the anchor for "Auto Row." In this *Oregon Journal* photograph, there is construction around the curbs, and a streetcar is passing going south. (Photograph courtesy of the *Oregonian*; Oregon Historical Society, 007715.)

Francis Ford's remodeled look is shown in this 1981 photograph. The windows around the ground floor were enlarged. The recession of the 1980s hit car dealerships hard across the country, and manufacturers had to step in to keep some afloat. Ford decided that it would prioritize the new suburban dealerships over the old-time central city stores. Francis Ford closed the doors on February 14, 1982. (City of Portland Archives, A2012-008.302.14.)

In 1982, the Benjamin Franklin Savings & Loan Association purchased the three-story auto dealership and incorporated it into a new six-story office building. Federal regulators closed Ben Franklin in 1990, and Multnomah County bought the building. The ground-floor openings that once held showroom windows frame an odd front porch for the county. Also, the Savings & Loan planned to add four additional floors later and knew that six elevators would be required for a 10-story building. They built six shafts, installed four cars, and left two shafts empty, which remain today. (Photograph by Richard Melling.)

The Walter F. Burrell residence, built in 1901 near the intersection of Twenty-seventh and Hawthorne Avenues, was designed by local architects Whidden and Lewis and is in the National Register of Historic Places. It shows the influence of Prairie-style architecture as practiced by Frank Lloyd Wright and has been compared to Wright's Joseph Husser House in Chicago. The mansion was built on 2.75 acres with 20 rooms, including a third-floor grand ballroom. The balcony on the third story provides expansive views to the west, as seen in this 1923 image. (Architectural Heritage Center.)

On July 7, 1920, osteopathic physicians F.E. and H.C.P. Moore purchased the home from the Burrell family and opened a sanitarium there, using "the milk and rest cure." As F.E. Moore explained to the Convention of Northwest Milk Inspectors in 1919, the cure was a four-week inpatient process where the patient's diet consists solely of two to eight quarts of raw milk per day. He told the inspectors that total bed rest was important for the first three weeks of the cure. This image is from a postcard promoting their business around 1922. (Gholston Collection.)

A room in the mansion is seen in this 1923 photograph. Walter Burrell was a very successful businessman and investor who lobbied for sidewalks and streetlights on Hawthorne Boulevard. The Burrells moved out in 1919 after their 14-year-old son Robert tragically died after swallowing strychnine crystals in the basement. (Architectural Heritage Center.)

First established on the west side in 1854, Holman's is the second-oldest continually operating business in the state of Oregon. Downtown congestion in the early 20th century led Holman's to seek quieter quarters in Northwest Portland, but neighborhood organizing led to city council rejections of two sites. On August 6, 1924, the Portland City Council spent the morning hearing protests from Southeast Portland residents before voting unanimously to grant the permit based on assurances that the natural beauty of the large property would be maintained and that landscaping would shield the mortuary business from the surrounding residences. The postcard view above shows Holman's Funeral Services in 1965, a few years before it sold half of the grounds for a new commercial development. The image below depicts a funeral in 1980. (Both, City of Portland Archives, A2004-002.6269 and A2012-008.114.15.)

From 1945 until his death in 1972, Carl "Doc" Severinsen practiced dentistry in a very small building at the southwest corner of Forty-second Avenue and Hawthorne Boulevard. His son was known as "Doc Jr." when he was growing up in the small town of Arlington, Oregon, in the eastern part of the state. When the child prodigy trumpet player hit the big time, the "Jr." was dropped. His long musical career has included the NBC orchestra and *The Tonight Show Starring Johnny Carson*. (Oregon Historical Society, OrHi 58686.)

Even after he became famous, Doc visited Oregon again and again. In 1963, he put on a trumpet clinic and an evening concert with Portland public school students at Cleveland High School. He played the Oregon State Fair in 1972. In 1985, he played with the Oregon Symphony Orchestra at the Arlene Schnitzer Concert Hall. His mother, Minnie, was often in the front row. (US Army Band.)

Martina Gangle Curl grew up working with her mother as a migrant fruit picker in Southwest Washington. In 1920, at the age of 14, she moved to Southeast Portland to live with her grandmother and attend Franklin High School where her artistic talents were noticed and supported. Later, she attended the Museum Art School. In 1936, she joined the Communist Party and got a job with the Works Progress Administration (WPA) Federal Art Project. She painted watercolors for display in the WPA-built Timberline Lodge on Mount Hood and won wide acclaim for her prints, sculptures, and murals. She is at work on a wood carving in this 1938 photograph. (City of Portland Archives, A2001-074.56.)

Never the bashful sort of communist, Martina, with her husband, Hank Curl, operated the John Reed Bookstore, which was on Hawthorne Boulevard from 1987 to 1992. It was named for Portland native John Reed, who, in recognition of his service to the Russian Revolution, is buried in the Kremlin Wall. In this 1941 photograph, Martina is in the lobby of the Multnomah Hotel with Capt. John Keegan of the Portland Police Red Squad. In spite of ongoing harassment by the police and the Federal Bureau of Investigation, Martina was a leader in the Union of Cultural Workers and the Workers Alliance of Oregon. (City of Portland Archives, A2001-074.22.)

Martina was a serial lawbreaker over five decades. In this 1985 photograph, she is being arrested in Southwest Washington for blocking the "white train," which was carrying nuclear weapons components. Martina and her friend and fellow radical Julia Ruuttila were arrested in 1973 at the offices of Pacific Power and Light while protesting high utility bills. When she was on trial for blocking the gates at the Trojan Nuclear Power Plant in 1976, she recalled her first such arrest in 1939 at the docks in Portland protesting shipments to imperial Japan. (Photograph by Max Gutierrez; Oregon Historical Society, 020031.)

Herman Pauling operated pharmacies in Condon and East Portland before he died unexpectedly in 1910 when his son Linus was 12. Left with three children to raise on her own, Belle Pauling sold their home and the pharmacy and purchased a 10-room boardinghouse on Hawthorne Avenue just east of Thirty-ninth Avenue. In this photograph Linus; his mother, Belle; and his sisters Lucile (left) and Pauline (right) pose in front of the boardinghouse in 1917. (Ava Helen and Linus Pauling Papers, Oregon State University Libraries.)

Linus Pauling is the only person to have ever won two unshared Nobel Prizes—one in 1954 for chemistry and one in 1962 for peace. He earned degrees from Oregon State University and Cal Tech and many honorary degrees. However, he left Washington High School in Southeast Portland without a diploma in 1916 because he was not allowed to take both semesters of American history at the same time. In 1962, Washington High decided he was qualified and issued him the diploma pictured above. (Ava Helen and Linus Pauling Papers, Oregon State University Libraries.)

Linus and Ava Helen Pauling met while they were both students at Oregon State University, and they worked very closely throughout their lives. Ava was a leader in the Women's International League for Peace and Freedom and a tireless campaigner for peace. Here, they are working on gathering the signatures of 13,000 scientists on a petition demanding an end to atomic weapons testing. When Linus accepted the Nobel Peace Prize for this petition, he noted that Ava's contribution was as important as his own. (Ava Helen and Linus Pauling Papers, Oregon State University Libraries.)

This sculpture is a tribute to Linus Pauling, and it stands in front of the house on Hawthorne Boulevard where the Paulings lived. In this 2009 photograph, a sign over the door reads, "Linus Pauling House." The sculpture *Alpha Helix* is by Julian Voss-Andreae, an internationally acclaimed sculptor who lives in Portland's Sellwood neighborhood. Voss-Andreae was a published scholar in quantum physics before he turned to sculpture. (Photograph by Owen Scholes.)

Linus and Ava are pictured here in the torchlight parade after the 1962 Nobel Awards. Eight years earlier, when he received his prize for chemistry, Linus was chosen to deliver an address to a large crowd of students after the traditional torchlight parade. He told them the following: "When an old and distinguished person speaks to you, listen to him carefully and with respect—but do not believe him. Never put your trust in anything but your own intellect. Your elder, no matter whether he has gray hair or has lost his hair, no matter whether he is a Nobel Laureate—may be wrong. The world progresses, year by year, century by century, as the members of the younger generation find out what was wrong among the things that their elders said. So, you must always be skeptical—always think for yourself." (Ava Helen and Linus Pauling Papers, Oregon State University Libraries.)

BIBLIOGRAPHY

Abbott, Carl. *Portland in Three Centuries*. Corvallis: Oregon State University Press, 2011.
———. *Portland: Urban Life and Landscape in the Pacific Northwest*. Philadelphia: University of Pennsylvania Press, 2001.
———. *The Great Extravaganza*. Portland: Oregon Historical Society, 1981.
DeMarco, Gordon. *A Short History of Portland*. San Francisco: Lexicos, 1990.
Hardyman, Rachel Ann. "Hawthorne Boulevard: Commercial Gentrification and the Creation of an Image." Portland: Portland State University thesis, 1992.
Johnson, Robert. *The Radical Middle Class: Populist Democracy and the Question of Capitalism in Progressive Era Portland, Oregon*. Princeton: Princeton University Press, 2003.
Leeson, Fred. *My-Te-Fine Merchant*. Portland: Irvington Press, 2014.
Lowenstein, Steve. *The Jews of Oregon, 1850–1950*. Portland: Jewish Historical Society of Portland, 1987.
MacColl, E. Kimbark, and Harry H. Stein. *Merchants Money and Power*. Portland: Georgian Press, 1988.
McLagan, Elizabeth. *A Peculiar Paradise: A History of Blacks in Oregon, 1788–1940*. Portland: Georgian Press, 1980.
Munk, Michael. *The Portland Red Guide*. Portland: Ooligan Press, 2011.
Oregon Black Pioneers and Kimberly Stowers Moreland. *African Americans of Portland*. Charleston: Arcadia Publishing, 2013.
oregonencyclopedia.org
Prince, Tracy J., and Zadie J. Schaffer. *Notable Women of Portland*. Charleston: Arcadia Publishing, 2017.
Wong, Marie Rose. *Sweet Cakes, Long Journey: The Chinatowns of Portland, Oregon*. Seattle: University of Washington Press, 2004.

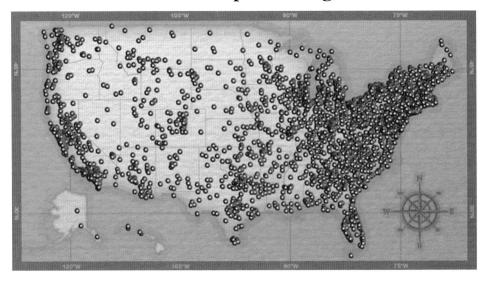